Easy English!

Series Editor

Adrian Wallwork
English for Academics SAS
Pisa, Italy

Easy English is a series of books intended for students and teachers of English as a foreign language.

More information about this series at http://www.springer.com/series/15586

Adrian Wallwork

Top 50 Grammar Mistakes

How to Avoid Them

Adrian Wallwork
English for Academics SAS
Pisa, Italy

ISSN 2522-8617   ISSN 2522-8625   (electronic)
Easy English!
ISBN 978-3-319-70983-3   ISBN 978-3-319-70984-0   (eBook)
https://doi.org/10.1007/978-3-319-70984-0

Library of Congress Control Number: 2017963153

Printed on acid-free paper

This Springer imprint is published by Springer Nature
The registered company is Springer International Publishing AG
The registered company address is: Gewerbestrasse 11, 6330 Cham, Switzerland

Contents

Part 2 Revision Tests

Student's Introduction

What Is Easy English?

Easy English is a series of books to help you learn and revise your English with minimal effort.
There are two main strands of the series. You can improve your English by

1. doing short exercises to improve specific areas of grammar (this book) and vocabulary. The grammar and vocabulary books on focus the areas that tend to lead to the most mistakes. The aim is just to highlight what you really need rather than overwhelming you with a mass of rules, many of which may have no practical daily value
2. reading texts in English that you might well normally read in your own language (e.g. personality tests, jokes, lateral thinking games, word searches).

Who Is this Book for? What Level Do I Need to Be?

Anyone who is interested in eliminating the typical mistakes they make as a result of not being able to easily distinguish between similar grammatical items (e.g. the difference between the present perfect and the simple past, or between that and which).

You need to have reached a mid-intermediate level of English to benefit from this book.

Which Is the Best Format to Buy this Book in?

Paper, without any doubt. The exercises involve you writing or underlining directly onto the page. With an e-reader this would be much more difficult. However, an e-book provides a dictionary which will occasionally be useful for you.

How Many Grammar Mistakes Are Dealt with?

This book is called *The Top 50 Grammar Mistakes*. In reality there are several hundred mistakes dealt within the 50 chapters of Part 1 of this book. The 50 chapters are grouped by type of mistake, rather than individual mistakes.

In What Sense Is this Book an Example of 'Easy English'?

Many books on grammar try to cover too much and appear to give equal coverage to grammatical rules irrespectively of whether these rules:

- are common
- frequently give rise to mistakes

This means that you can end up doing many exercises that will not really be of much benefit to you. This is because they practise rules and examples that you are unlikely to meet in real life.

This book thus focuses on the areas of English grammar that tend to give rise to the most mistakes.

It is 'easy' because

- the typical mistakes are clearly laid out and easy to read
- example sentences contain examples using common English vocabulary
- the exercises are quick to do (they just involve underlining the correct answer) and they are quick to check

Of course, English can be much more complex. The good news is that the complex areas of English grammar are also those that tend to be used the least.

How Is the Book Organized?

Each chapter has a HEADING which gives the key words dealt with in the section. In the explanations below I will be referring to Chapter 32 (*Much, Many, A Lot of, Lots of*).

Each chapter is made up of five subsections.

1) THE FIRST SUBSECTION shows some typical mistakes. All sentences in *italics* are mistakes. Each mistake is then followed in the line below with the correct version (in normal script). The key point is highlighted in bold in the correct version. Here is an example:

Was there much people?
Were there **many** people?

2) In the SECOND SUBSECTION correct examples are given of the key words used in typical situations. These correct examples are shown in a box with a grey background. Here is an example:

> We have **a lot of** information.
>
> We **do not** have **much** information.

3) In the THIRD SUBSECTION, very simple guidelines are given of the key words. For example:

Guidelines

- **much** - used with UNCOUNTABLE NOUNS, generally in negative and interrogative.
- **many** - used with plural nouns, generally in negative and interrogative
- **a lot of** - used with all nouns, typically in the affirmative but also in the interrogative
- **lots of** - can replace *a lot of* in affirmative, but is not suitable for formal situations. **lots of** is very rarely used in negative phrases, and is also quite rare in questions.

These guidelines are not comprehensive, they are designed to give you a quick easy-to-remember guideline to the most common uses of the particular word in question.

4) In the FOURTH SUBSECTION, there is an exercise which tests the key words given in the heading of the chapter, so in this case **much, many, a lot of, lots of**.

The exercise simply consists in underlining the correct form. In some cases, more than one form may be correct. Here is an example:

1. I have **a lot of / lots of / many / much** books on this subject.

2. We have **a lot of homework / much homework / many homeworks** to do tonight.

In question 1) *a lot of, lots of* and *many* are all possible answers, so you should underline all three. In question 2) only *a lot of homework* is possible.

A few of the exercises are based on exercises that can be found in English for Academic Research: Grammar Exercises (Springer), which is part of a series of books on academic English, whereas the book you are reading now is focused on general English.

5) The FINAL SUBSECTION is the key. If a form is written in brackets, this means that this form is possible but that the form not in brackets is more common. For example:

18) a lot of advice 19) much (a lot of) 20) much feedback

The best answer to question 19) is *much* but *a lot of* would also be possible.

Revision Tests

In Part 2 of the book there are two sets of revision test. Revision Tests 1 deals all the incorrect sentences given in the first subsection of each chapter. Correct the sentences, then go to the first subsection of the relevant chapter to see the answer. Revision Tests 2 is based on the second subsection of each chapter. Again, go to the second subsection of the relevant chapter to see the answer.

For example:

The test on page 152 looks likes this.

1. I have much work at the moment.
2. How much times have you been there?
3. Was there much people?
4. You don't need many money to do this.

In the above case, you correct the sentences. Then to check your answers, turn to page 87, where you will see the same sentences (this time in *italics*) but with the correct answers below (in normal script).

I have much work at the moment.

I have **a lot of** work at the moment.

How much times have you been there?

How **many** times have you been there?

Was there much people?

Were there **many** people?

You don't need many money to do this.

You don't need **much / a lot of** money to do this.

Where Can I Find More Grammar Explanations and Tests?

Top 50 grammar mistakes is aimed at students studying general English. I have also written a series of books on academic English.

If you want more detailed grammar explanations, then you can find them in this book:

English for Research: Grammar, Usage and Style https://link.springer.com/book/10.1007/978-1-4614-1593-0

If you would like to do extra grammar exercises and see examples of English sentences in a more technical context, then you can use this book:

English for Academic Research: Grammar Exercises https://link.springer.com/book/10.1007/978-1-4614-1593-0

The companion to *Top 50 grammar mistakes* which is entitled *Top 50 vocabulary mistakes* also contains many exercises that you might find useful.

By using all these books in combination, your level of English should improve considerably.

In the appendix, you can find the index to the *Grammar Exercises* and the Table of Contents of the *Vocabulary Exercises* book. This will help you to find additional grammar explanations or exercises.

What Are the Other Books in this Series? Which One Should I Read Next?

Currently there are five other books in the series.

Top 50 vocabulary mistakes - how to avoid them

Wordsearches - widen your vocabulary in English

Test your personality - quizzes that are fun and improve your English

Word games, riddles and logic tests - boost your English and have fun

Jokes - have a laugh and improve your English

Apart from the vocabulary book, the other four books are designed to be dipped into rather than being read from the first page to the last. 'Dipped into' means that you can pick up the book and read any page you like, and for as long as you like.

You are likely to have more fun with the books if you read two or three at the same time. So rather than spending the next month concentrating exclusively on vocabulary or grammar, you might find it more fun and stimulating to read a few jokes from the Jokes book, and do a few wordsearches and quizzes.

Teachers Introduction

Which Grammar Mistakes Were Chosen and Why?

You might expect learners of English whose native languages are different (e.g. Arabic, Japanese, Polish, Spanish) to make very different mistakes when writing and reading in English. In reality, while there are some mistakes that that are unique to a particular language speaker, there is a core of mistakes that ALL non-native speakers make. For example, speakers of virtually all the world's main languages will say something similar to *I am here since a week* instead of *I have been here (for) a week*.

The aim of this book and its companion book on vocabulary (Top 50 vocabulary mistakes - how to avoid them) is to focus on the most commonly made mistakes. This means that readers can set themselves a reasonable target. So rather than trying to learn all English grammar and learning interminably long lists of words, students (and you the teacher) can just focus on those areas / words that tend to be used the most frequently and / or tend to create the most misunderstandings.

This approach (focus on key issues only) immediately differentiates the two books from already existing books on the market (grammars, and grammar / vocabulary exercise books) whose coverage is far too wide or whose aim is simply for reference.

I consulted books of typical mistakes made by speakers of some of the most important languages in the world: Chinese, French, Italian, German, Japanese, Portuguese, Russian and Spanish. I also had access to mistakes made by Czechs, Poles, and Romanians. I then looked to see what mistakes in English were common to the majority of these languages. You can find a list of these books on page xi of the companion volume *Top 50 vocabulary mistakes*.

I was somewhat hampered by the fact that one of the two books I had on Chinese mistakes and the only book I could find on Japanese mistakes were in the native languages, and I was thus only able to read the sentences in English. I am also influenced by the fact that I live and teach in Italy, and therefore have a natural tendency towards noticing and recording mistakes by speakers of Latinate languages - French, Portuguese, Romanian and Spanish. Thus I would say that my book suffers from a bias of containing more 'European' mistakes than any other.

In any case, all the mistakes listed in this book and in its companion book on Vocabulary mistakes are extremely common. If your students manage to master the differences between the various words and constructions, then their English will improve massively - much more so than trying to learn all English vocabulary or all grammar items.

What Is the Main Focus and Rationale?

I have tried to focus on those grammar mistakes that non-native English speakers of all languages tend to make, i.e. those mistakes that are common to speakers of all language groups, whether they be, for instance, French, Russian, or Chinese.

Clearly, mistakes tend to vary from language speaker to language speaker, but there does seem to be a core of typical mistakes as I discovered by researching the books on typical mistakes.

However, there are some areas of grammar that tend to be more idiosyncratic and these are:

- word order - i.e. the position of the main parts of the sentence: subject, verb, object; and also the position of adverbs
- prepositions

Word order and the use of preposition tends to vary massively from language to language, even languages within the same language group, and of course some languages don't even have prepositions.

I have not gone into massive detail about the differences between the various tenses, as in any case this would have required a lot of space.

Instead I have tried to only focus on those errors that cause the most mistakes. This means that within a certain category, e.g. the definite article or the present perfect, I have not covered every single possible rule and mistake. The idea is to promote 'easy English' which means ignoring anything too complex, unless it is a frequent source of error.

I have also avoided areas that tend to lead to confusing explanations (*be used to vs get used to*; some uses of the present continuous and present perfect continuous; anomalous uses of *some* and *any*) or are only useful in the written form (*which* vs *that*). Some of these more complex items can be found in the books listed below in the section entitled: *Where can I find more grammar explanations and tests?*

How Should I Use this book?

The exercises in this book can be used to test student's proficiency with particular sets of words with similar meanings.

They are best used after a specific mistake has been made by a student. For example, if a student misuses *make* and *let*, and you believe that this is a recurrent mistake or is likely to be made by others in the class, then you can:

- write the mistake on the whiteboard
- refer students to the explanation of the differences - example sentences are highlighted in a grey background in each section, and are followed by guidelines to usage
- check your students' understanding - in a monolingual class, you can give them a few examples in their own language for them to translate.
- give them the exercise

A few lessons later you can then revise the point, by giving students the relevant exercise from the exercise contained in Part 2 Revision Tests.

Where Can I Find More Grammar Explanations and Tests?

If you want more detailed grammar explanations, then you can find them in this book:

English for Research: Grammar, Usage and Style https://link.springer.com/book/10.1007/978-1-4614-1593-0

If you would like to do extra grammar exercises and see examples of English sentences in a more technical context, then you can use this book:

English for Academic Research: Grammar Exercises https://link.springer.com/book/10.1007/978-1-4614-1593-0

The companion to *Top 50 grammar mistakes*, which is entitled *Top 50 vocabulary mistakes*, also contains many exercises that you might find useful.

By using all these books in combination, your level of English should improve considerably.

In the appendix, you can find the index to the *Grammar Exercises* and the Table of Contents of the *Vocabulary Exercises* book. This will help you to find additional grammar explanations or exercises.

Author's Request to Teachers

It would be great if you could contribute to future editions. Please send me examples or explanations that you would like me to include. Please be as specific as possible, provide clear examples, and highlight to me why you think the 'mistake' should be included.

Please also let me know if you find any typos or explanations and keys to exercises that you don't agree with.

Finally, feel free to contact me (adrian.wallwork@gmail.com) if you have ideas for other books that could be part of this Easy English series.

Please also check out our self published books at: sefl.co.uk

About the Author

Since 1984 I have been teaching English as a foreign language - from General English to Business English to Scientific English. I have taught students of all nationalities, and this book is based primarily on the typical mistakes that these students make. I am the author of over 30 textbooks for Springer Science+Business Media, Cambridge University Press, Oxford University Press, the BBC, and many other publishers.

Part 1
Top 50 Grammar Mistakes

Chapter 1
Advise, Recommend, Suggest

Can you suggest me a place to go?

Can you suggest **a place for me to go**? / **where I should go**?

I advise to see a lawyer.

I **(would) advise you to see** a lawyer.

He recommended her to see a doctor.

He recommended that **she should see** a doctor.

I recommend to identify some key points to remember.

I **recommend that we should identify / recommend identifying** some key points to remember.

We suggest you to come with us.

We suggest (that) you (should) come with us.

They suggested to use Google Translate.

They suggested **using** Google Translate.

© Springer International Publishing AG 2018
A. Wallwork, *Top 50 Grammar Mistakes*, Easy English!,
https://doi.org/10.1007/978-3-319-70984-0_1

"Why don't you see a doctor?"

He suggested / recommended **(that) she (should) see** a doctor.

He advised **her to see** a doctor.

I would advise **you to see** a doctor.

Have you thought about seeing a doctor? It might be a good idea to see a doctor.

"Why don't we all go out for a drink?"

He suggested that **we should all go** out for a drink.

He suggested **we all go** out for a drink.

He suggested **going** out for a drink.

"What can I do? Where can I go?"

Can you suggest / recommend **what I could do** and **where I could go**?

Can you suggest / recommend **somewhere (for me) to go**?

Can you advise **me where to go**?

Guidelines

- **suggest doing something**. This form tends to be used when the subject of *suggest* is also involved in the activity. e.g. *He suggested going for a coffee =* he is going for a coffee with the others.
- **suggest (that) someone (should) do something**. This form tends to be used when the subject of *suggest* is making the suggestion to someone else. e.g. *They suggested that I should go and see a doctor.* However, it can also be used when the person making the suggestion is also going to be involved in the activity e.g. *He suggested that we should all go and get a coffee.*
- **recommend** follows the same rules as **suggest**
- **recommend something / someone to someone**: *He recommended his lawyer to me.* Not: He recommended to me his lawyer.
- **advise someone to do something** e.g. *They advised us to go by train.*

Choose the correct form

1. What do you suggest **that I should do / me to do**?
2. They advised **to get / us to get** there early.
3. Health experts recommend **reducing / to reduce / that we reduce** our intake of salt.
4. He advised **seeing / me to see** his dentist.
5. I suggest **you to go / that you should go** there.
6. He recommended **to me a bar on the high street / a bar on the high street (to me).**
7. We suggest **doing / to do** this at least once a day.
8. I **recommend to follow / following** these instructions very carefully.
9. I suggest **you to study / you should study** more.
10. They advised **to not have contact / us not to have contact** with her again.

1) that I should do 2) us to get 3) that we reduce / reducing 4) me to see 5) that you should 6) a bar on the high street to me 7) doing 8) following 9) you should study 10) us not to have contact

Chapter 2
Allow, Enable, Permit, Let

It is not allowed / permitted to smoke in class.

Smoking is not permitted in class. / **You are not allowed to smoke** in class.

The teacher lets us to talk during lessons.

The teacher **lets us talk** during lessons.

They allow using the dictionary during the exam.

They **allow you to use** a dictionary during the exam.

This enables to make multiple copies.

This **enables multiple copies to be made**.

It is not permitted walking on the grass.

Walking on the grass **is not permitted**. / **Don't walk** on the grass.

© Springer International Publishing AG 2018
A. Wallwork, *Top 50 Grammar Mistakes*, Easy English!,
https://doi.org/10.1007/978-3-319-70984-0_2

> Our parents **let us go** to bed late.
>
> The teacher **allowed / permitted us to use** a calculator during the exam.
>
> This app **enables / permits / allows you to order** a taxi.
>
> This **app lets you order** a taxi.
>
> They were **allowed / permitted to go** home early.

Guidelines

- All these verbs have the same meaning, though **let** is the least formal and **permit** the most formal. **enable** cannot be used when giving permission but only in the sense of facilitating.
- They all require a personal object (e.g. to allow *someone / you / her* to do something).
- **let** is less formal, requires the infinitive without *to*, and is not used in the passive form.

Choose the correct form

1. Her parents **allowed her do / allowed her doing** anything she wanted.
2. Social networks **enable people / enable** to reach a wider audience, thus **enabling them to share / enabling them sharing** opinions.
3. The new law **permits shops to trade / permits to trade** 24 hours a day
4. These binoculars **let you see / let you to see** for miles.
5. They were not permitted **leave / to leave / leaving** the country.
6. This kind of behavior is not **permitted / permitting**.
7. This software enables calculations **to make / to be made** more quickly.
8. This system **allows to save / allows you to save** a lot of money.
9. This will **allow / allow us** to make more money.
10. She didn't **let them to watch / let them watch** Netflix.

1) allowed her to do 2) enable people, enabling them to share 3) permits shops to trade 4) let you see 5) to leave 6) permitted 7) to be made 8) allows you to save 9) allow us 10) let them watch

Chapter 3
Already, Just, Still, Yet

Are you just here? You are a little early, aren't you?

Are you **already** here? You are a little early, aren't you?

Are you yet here? I thought you had gone.

Are you **still** here? I thought you had gone.

I haven't yet decided what to do.

I haven't decided what to do **yet**.

They haven't still come - I am worried about them.

They **still** haven't come - I am worried about them.

They are here yet.

They are here **already**.

© Springer International Publishing AG 2018
A. Wallwork, *Top 50 Grammar Mistakes*, Easy English!,
https://doi.org/10.1007/978-3-319-70984-0_3

Is it midnight **already**? Time for bed then.

Is it midnight **yet**? I can't wait to open the champagne to celebrate the new year.

Have you finished **already**? It didn't take you very long.

Have you finished **yet**? You seem to be taking a long time.

They have **already** arrived. Typical, they always arrive early.

They have **just** arrived. Go help them with their suitcases.

They haven't arrived **yet**. But I imagine they will be here soon in any case.

They **still** haven't arrived. Where are they? I hope they haven't had an accident.

Guidelines

already + the affirmative: an event has taken place which may or may not be surprising (*I have already seen this film so I don't want to see it again* - neutral; *ten students have come already,* I was only expecting six).

already + the interrogative: the questioner expresses some surprise (*I saw their car in the outside. Are they already here?*) or great surprise (*Heavens! Are they back already? I thought they were going to be at least two hours*). Note that the position of *already* in the phrase indicates the level of surprise.

yet + the interrogative: the questioner wants to know if an event has taken place or not, there is no urgency or surprise involved (*Are they here yet?*). By making the question negative the questioner adds a sense of surprise (*Aren't they here yet?*)

yet + the negative: a simple statement that something has not happened within the expected time frame (*They haven't finished yet.*)

still: the speaker is surprised in the **interrogative** (*Are they still here? I thought they would be gone by now*) and either neutral or surprised in the **affirmative** (*They are still here. When are they going to go?*)

just + affirmative only: refers to an event that happened very recently (*They have just left - only a couple of minutes ago in fact*)

Note: Consult a good grammar to learn about the correct position for all these words (*already, just, still, yet*) and what tenses to use as these differ between US and GB English. For the sake of space and simplicity, the exercises below just test the meaning of the words.

Choose the correct form

1. I thought it was unusual that they hadn't **already / just / still / yet** been told.
2. I thought it was unusual that they hadn't been told **already / just / still / yet**.
3. You **already / just / still / yet** haven't told me about your holiday.
4. He has **already / just / still / yet** got back from India so he's suffering from a bit of jet lag.
5. I have **already / just / still / yet** been on the phone to Mary - she's pregnant!
6. I have **already / just / still / yet** called them twice this morning - where are they?
7. Message on phone: Are you there **already / just / still / yet**? If you have arrived, can you give me a call?
8. Message on phone: Are you **already / just / still / yet** at home? If you haven't left yet, could you get my book from beside the bed and bring it with you?
9. Have you done your homework **already / just / still / yet?** You know we are going out tonight so you really need to finish it now.
10. Have you **already / just / still / yet** done your homework? How did you manage to do it so fast?
11. I am not sure if I have **already / just / still / yet** told you, but I have decided to get a new job.
12. I am not sure if I have told you **already / just / still / yet**, but I have decided to get a new job.

1) already 2) yet (already) 3) still 4) just 5) just 6) already 7) yet 8) still 9) yet 10) already 11) already 12) yet (already)

Chapter 4
Articles: *A, An*

She has a Apple computer.

She has **an** Apple computer.

He has an university degree and a MBA.

He has **a** university degree and **an** MBA.

He was driving without license.

He was driving without **a** license.

She works in bank.

She works in **a** bank.

I came without ID.

I came without any ID / an identity card / an ID.

© Springer International Publishing AG 2018
A. Wallwork, *Top 50 Grammar Mistakes*, Easy English!,
https://doi.org/10.1007/978-3-319-70984-0_4

> This is **a** European law.
>
> This is **an** EU law.
>
> This is **a** universal problem.
>
> This is **an u**nusual problem.
>
> He is **an** NBC player.
>
> He is **a n**otoriously good player.
>
> You cannot enter the country without **a** visa or **a** permit.
>
> I need **(some)** information about how to ...

Guidelines

- The difference between **a** and **an** is not grammatical, but is simply based on sound. Use *a* before every consonant, unless this consonant is part of an acronym where the letter in the acronym has a vowel sound (e.g. F = eff, M = em, N = en).
- **an** is used before *u*, if the *u* is pronounced as in *uncle, understanding, uninteresting.*
- **a** is used before *u*, if the sound is like you e.g. *university, unique, utility*
- **a** is used before *eu*
- **a** is used before *h* except in these cases*: an hour, an honor, an honest, an heir*
- **a** and **an** are called 'indefinite articles'. All countable nouns in the singular require an article (either **a / an** or **the**). You cannot say, for example, ~~I am without ticket~~. But instead you should say *I don't have a ticket* or *the ticket.*
- If a noun is uncountable, then *a / an* are not used. You cannot say ~~I need an information~~, instead you can use *some* or *a piece of* or in some cases simply omit the article.

Choose the correct form. Note: Ø = no article required

1. You can't go there without **a / Ø** passport.
2. We climbed **a / an / Ø** high mountain.
3. I would like **a / an / some** information.
4. I speak **a / an / Ø** good English.
5. It travels at 90 km **a / an / Ø** hour.
6. I have **a / an / Ø** headache.
7. It is spelt with **a / an** L, not **a / an** R.
8. We went to **a / an** hotel.
9. He gave me **a / Ø** good feedback on my work.
10. It is **a / an** MP3 file - I haven't seen one of those for **a / an** year or more.

1) a 2) a 3) some 4) Ø 5) an 6) a 7) an, an 8) a 9) Ø 10) an, a

Chapter 5
Articles: *A / An* vs *One* vs *It* vs Genitive

Do you have one mobile phone? Yes, I have it.

Do you have **a** mobile phone? Yes, I have **one**.

Do you think that this year will be more active than the last one?

Do you think that this year will be more active than **last year**?

That isn't David's umbrella, the one of David is striped.

That isn't David's umbrella, **David's** is striped.

We didn't go to Sigmund's house, we went to the one of Petra.

We didn't go to Sigmund's house, we went to **Petra's**.

Bill and Mary went to the movies. This one had already seen it.

Bill and Mary went to the movies. **Bill** had already seen it.

© Springer International Publishing AG 2018
A. Wallwork, *Top 50 Grammar Mistakes*, Easy English!,
https://doi.org/10.1007/978-3-319-70984-0_5

> I have bought **a** new car - it is self-driving.
>
> They have two cars. She has **one** and her husband has **one**.
>
> I went to the shop to buy the new iPhone and I bought the last **one**.
>
> Do you have a self-driving car? Yes, I have **one**.
>
> Do you have **it** with you now? Yes, I do.
>
> Have you found your mobile? Yes I have found **it**.
>
> Their two children - Jay and Kay - came with them. **Jay** is only five months' old.
>
> This **one** is bigger than that **one**.

Guidelines

- **a / an** refer to a generic item, **one** is a number and means a single item rather than two or three.
- do not use *the one of* to refer to an object belonging to a person (e.g. *this is Adrian's*; not ~~this is the one of Adrian~~).
- **it** refers to a particular item not to a generic item.
- English tends to repeat the noun rather than using *one* to replace the second mention of the noun. However there are exceptions to this general rule.
- **one** can be used in comparisons when the object in question has already been established.
- **this / that one** are not used to refer back to people, instead repeat the name of the person.

Choose the correct form

1. Do you have a self driving car? Yes I have **it / one**.
2. There were **a / one** hundred people not two hundred.
3. We only did **a / one** test before the machine broke down.
4. I don't have my car with me but we can use **the one of Anna / Anna's**.
5. All these lamps need just **a / one** bulb. For this lamp we need **an / one** 80 watt bulb and for this lamp **a / one** 60 watt bulb.
6. I like both these pictures. This **one / picture** looks like a Matisse and that **one / picture** looks like a Picasso.
7. We are going to Paris this year and Rome **the next one / next year**.
8. I went to **a / one** university in England.

1) one 2) one 3) one 4) Anna's 5) one, an, a 6) one / picture, one / picture 7) next year 8) a

Chapter 6
Articles: *The* vs Zero Article (Ø)

All you need is the love.

All you need **is love**.

English were very shortsighted to initiate Brexit.

The English were very shortsighted to initiate Brexit.

The drug is a serious problem in today's society.

Drugs are a serious problem in today's society.

He had short hair and the eyes were brown.

He had short hair and **his** eyes were brown.

© Springer International Publishing AG 2018   17
A. Wallwork, *Top 50 Grammar Mistakes*, Easy English!,
https://doi.org/10.1007/978-3-319-70984-0_6

> Make **love** not **war**.
>
> **The love** she felt for him did not waver while he was away during **the war** in Afghanistan.
>
> **Researchers** spend a lot of time in **the laboratory**.
>
> **Pollution** is a serious environmental issue and **the pollution** we have here in China is about the worst in **the** world.
>
> **English** is spoken all around **the** world. **The English** themselves only represent about 10% of **native English speaking people**.

Guidelines

- **zero article (Ø)** - to refer to something in general (*a shortage of <u>water</u> could be the cause of the next world war*).
- **definite article (*the*)** - to refer to something specific (*we went for a swim at the sea, <u>the water</u> was very polluted*).
- **the** is generally not used with parts of the body (*move your left arm*).
- **the** is not usually used with languages, but **the** is used with nationalities - see Chapter 29.

Choose the correct form

1. I was **the / Ø** best student in **the / Ø** class.
2. I love **the / Ø** music. **The / Ø** type of **the / Ø** music that I love the most is **the / Ø** jazz.
3. This is **the / Ø** story of my life.
4. I work at **the / Ø** Department of **the / Ø** Engineering at **the / Ø** University of Tokyo in **the / Ø** Japan.
5. **The / Ø** change in the climate has significantly affected **the / Ø** environment.
6. **The / Ø** climate change has significantly depleted **the / Ø** ozone layer.
7. We saw **the / Ø** film at **the / Ø** cinema.
8. We found a great site on **the / Ø** Internet.
9. Using this toothpaste totally prevents **the / Ø** formation of **the / Ø** plaque.
10. Does **the / your** leg hurt?

1) the, the 2) Ø, the, Ø, Ø 3) the 4) the, Ø, the, Ø 5) the, the 6) Ø, the 7) the, the 8) the, Ø 9) Ø 10) your

Chapter 7
Be Able, Manage vs *Can / Could*

I am not able to decide which sentence is correct.

I **can't** decide which sentence is correct.

I have never can ski.

I **have never been able to** ski.

I will can pass the exam if I study.

I **will be able to** pass the exam if I study.

It was a very long marathon but she could reach the end.

It was a very long marathon but she **managed to reach** the end.

By searching the web, I could find all the info I needed.

By searching the web, I **managed to find / was able to find** all the info I needed.

© Springer International Publishing AG 2018
A. Wallwork, *Top 50 Grammar Mistakes*, Easy English!,
https://doi.org/10.1007/978-3-319-70984-0_7

> I would like **to be able to** speak Spanish but I **have never been able to** learn it.
>
> When I was five I **could** swim very well.
>
> When I lived in Manchester I **could** go and see the best concerts whenever I wanted to.
>
> We **couldn't** see because of the rain.
>
> I **couldn't** answer any of the questions.

Guidelines

- **can** has no form for the infinitive, present perfect, past perfect or continuous forms, instead a form of *to be able* is used.
- **could** can be used in the conditional e.g. *If I had time I could probably do it.*
- **could not** can be used to express incapacity in the past e.g. *I broke my leg in the accident so I couldn't move.*
- with reference to the past you cannot use **could** (in the affirmative or interrogative). For a specific occasion use **managed** or **was able to** e.g. *I managed / was able to answer all the questions in the test.*
- **could** with a past meaning can only be used for a repeated / habitual ability e.g. *I could play the piano when I was nine.*

Choose the correct form

1. I **could / am able to** be wrong, but I don't think so.
2. I will **can / be able to** tell you tomorrow.
3. He **can / is able to** speak ten languages.
4. I hope to **can / be able** to see her tomorrow.
5. We only had three days in London but we **could / managed to** see many places.
6. **Could you / Did you manage to** answer question 5?
7. When I was only three years old I **could / managed to** ride a bicycle - in fact I used to cycle to kindergarten with my mother.
8. She has never **could / been able** to do this.
9. If I knew the answer I **was able to / could** tell you.
10. I **could / am able to / manage to** sit here all day talking to you.
11. When I was young I **could / managed to / was able to** go out whenever I wanted.

1) could 2) be able to 3) can 4) be able 5) managed to 6) did you manage to (could you) 7) could 8) been able 9) could 10) could 11) could

Chapter 8
Be Born, Die

I am born in Rome.

I **was born** in Rome.

She is born in March so she is a Pisces.

She **was** born in March so she is a Pisces.

The baby will born next week.

The baby **will be born** next week.

They found him alone in the flat - he was died.

They found him alone in the flat - he was **dead**.

He was dead ten days ago.

He **had died** ten days ago.

She is dead since many years.

She **has been dead** for many years.

© Springer International Publishing AG 2018
A. Wallwork, *Top 50 Grammar Mistakes*, Easy English!,
https://doi.org/10.1007/978-3-319-70984-0_8

She **was born** in 1997.

Her baby **will be born** in a couple of months.

He **is** dead. He **died** last year. He **has been dead** for one year.

By the time the ambulance got to the scene of the accident he **was already dead**.

He **died** a few minutes before the ambulance arrived.

Guidelines

- **to be born** - note that *born* is preceded by a part of the verb *to be* (*is, will be, was* etc).
- when talking about your own birth or that of someone use the past tense of **to be** not the present (she *was* born).
- **to die** is a regular verb, it does not require the verb *to be*.
- **died** is the past tense of *to die*.
- **to be dead** - *dead* is an adjective and is the opposite of *alive*.
- remember to use the present perfect to refer to something that took place in the past and is still true today (*she had been dead for several years* - not: * *she is dead for several years*).

Choose the correct form

1. I **am born / was born** on a Tuesday, which apparently is supposed to be a lucky day.
2. He **was died / had died** before I **born / was born**.
3. How long **are they died / have they been dead**?
4. The child **will be born / will born** in hospital rather than at home.
5. He is **dead / died** - there is nothing we can do about it now.
6. When **is the baby born / will the baby be born**?
7. She **has been dead / is died** for many years.
8. Is she **dead / died**?

1) was born 2) had died, was born 3) have they been dead 4) will be born 5) dead 6) will the baby be born 7) has been dead 8) dead

Chapter 9
Be Going To

According to the forecast, it rains later this afternoon.

According to the forecast, it **is going to rain** later this afternoon.

Do you tell me or not?

Are you going to tell me or not?

How do I eat this without a knife and fork?

How **am I going to eat** this without a knife and fork?

When I get home I am making dinner and watching TV.

When I get home **I am going to make dinner and watch** TV.

Will you have a shower? If not, I am going to clean the bathroom now.

Are you going to have a shower? If not, I am going to clean the bathroom now.

© Springer International Publishing AG 2018
A. Wallwork, *Top 50 Grammar Mistakes*, Easy English!,
https://doi.org/10.1007/978-3-319-70984-0_9

> The piano is being delivered this afternoon. I don't know where **I am going to put** it.
>
> Tonight I **am just going to relax** in front of the TV.
>
> She says **she's going to be** a doctor when she grows up.
>
> Sorry but I **am not going to tell** you now. Maybe I'll find the courage to tell you tomorrow.
>
> According to the Bank of England, inflation **is going to rise** 2% next year.

Guidelines

- Use **going to** to refer to plans and intentions that we have already made decisions about. Examples: *He's going to change job next year.* (He has already decided to do this) *Are you going to see the Louvre while you're in Paris?* (Is this part of your planned itinerary?)
- Use **going to** to make predictions based on present or past evidence. In some cases we can already see that something is starting to happen. Examples: Look – it's going to rain. (*The clouds are black.*) She is not going to like these changes to the schedules. (*Past experience shows she doesn't like changes.*)
- For more info on this topic, see Chapter 50.

Choose the correct form

1. I **will / am going to** take a nap now - so please don't disturb me.
2. I **am taking / going to take** up yoga - I really need to be more relaxed.
3. You are **loving / going to love** Rome, it's absolutely beautiful.
4. **Is this going to take / Is this taking** a long time, because I really need to go out?
5. I'm sorry to hear the situation is so bad, but don't worry **I will / am going to** call her and see if I can resolve the matter for you.
6. New things **are going to / will** happen at this company, some of which you are not **liking / going to like**.
7. **Are they going to / Will they** play the music this loud all night?
8. When **are they finishing / going to finish** painting your apartment?
9. She has no money, so how **is she paying / going to pay** her medical bills when she starts her therapy?
10. After last night's argument is she **seeing / going to see** him again?

1) am going to 2) going to take 3) going to love 4) is this going to take 5) will 6) are going to, going to like 7) are they going to 8) going to finish 9) going to pay 10) going to see

Chapter 10
Be vs *Have*

It's snowing outside and I have cold.

It's snowing outside and I **am** cold.

She has 10 years.

She **is** 10 years old.

What day do we have today?

What day **is it** today?

You have right.

You **are** right.

Is there a computer at you?

Do you have a computer?

© Springer International Publishing AG 2018
A. Wallwork, *Top 50 Grammar Mistakes*, Easy English!,
https://doi.org/10.1007/978-3-319-70984-0_10

> She **is** three years old.
>
> You **are** right and I **am** wrong.
>
> I **am cold** - what's the temperature in here?
>
> I **have a cold**, in fact I think I am getting a temperature.

Guidelines

- **to be** is used rather than **to have** in the following situations: *to be + right, wrong, cold, hot, thirsty, hungry.*
- **to be** is used in relation to ages: *He is 45 years old.*
- **to have** is also used as an auxiliary verb to form the present perfect and past perfect of every verb, whether it is transitive or intransitive. **to be** is only used as an auxiliary to form the passive. For more on this see Chapter 11.

Choose the correct form

1. Do you have anything to drink? I **have / am** thirsty.
2. I **am / have** always cold when I go skiing.
3. We are having a party, do you want to come? Sorry, but I **am / have** a cold.
4. He **has / is** 70 years old tomorrow.
5. She **is / has** the same age as me.
6. I **am hungry / have hunger** - what's for dinner?
7. What date **do we have / is it** today?
8. She **is / has** very talented and I **am / have** jealous.

1) am 2) am 3) have 4) is 5) is 6) am hungry 7) is it 8) is, am

Chapter 11
Be vs *Have* as Auxiliary Verbs

Demand is decreased.

Demand **has** decreased.

He is gone back to the hotel.

He **has** gone back to the hotel.

She was arrived an hour before.

She **was** arrived an hour before.

The lecture is begun.

The lecture **has** begun.

Your child is grown a lot.

Your child **has** grown a lot.

Your English is improved.

Your English **has** improved.

The director had made to resign.

The director **was** made to resign.

© Springer International Publishing AG 2018
A. Wallwork, *Top 50 Grammar Mistakes*, Easy English!,
https://doi.org/10.1007/978-3-319-70984-0_11

The criminal **was arrested** by the police.

The police **had already arrested** the criminal twice before.

The project **was finished** on time.

The project **had already finished** when I joined the team.

Taxes **were increased** by 20% by the new government.

The problems **have increased** over the last two years.

The patient **was taken** to hospital in an ambulance.

The father **had taken** the children to school.

Guidelines

- *is / was / will be* etc + **past participle** - passive form (*the child was caught smoking* - it is not the child that does the action of catching but the teacher).
- *has / have / had* + **past participle** passive form (*the teacher had already caught the child smoking several times before* - the teacher does the action of catching).
- for more on this topic see Chapter 36.

Choose the correct form

1. He **has / is** gone home.
2. It **has / is** rained again.
3. For man years public interest **has / is** focused on water scarcity rather than the use of fossil fuels.
4. These goods **have / are** produced in India.
5. My friends **have / are** been to San Francisco.
6. The post **has / is** arrived.
7. **Had / were** you stayed there before?
8. **Have / Are** you come alone?
9. The project **had / was** terminated by the organizers due to lack of funding.
10. The price of petrol **has / is** gone up.
11. A lot of money **had / was** raised by crowdfunding.
12. She **had / was** seen shoplifting.

1) has 2) has 3) has 4) are 5) have 6) has 7) have 8) have 9) was 10) has 11) was 12) was

Chapter 12
Been vs *Gone*

I have gone to New York twice, the first time was in 2018.

I have **been** to New York twice, the first time was in 2018.

He had already gone there, so he didn't want to go again.

He had already **been** there, so he didn't want to go again.

Have you ever gone to Paris?

Have you ever **been** to Paris?

I have never gone to Venice.

I have never **been** to Venice.

You are late where have you gone?

You are late where have you **been**?

© Springer International Publishing AG 2018

A. Wallwork, *Top 50 Grammar Mistakes*, Easy English!,

https://doi.org/10.1007/978-3-319-70984-0_12

> He has **gone** to China - I don't suppose we'll see him again for a long time.
>
> He has **been** to China twice. He said it was fascinating and he can't wait to go back.
>
> We had **gone** home already, that's why you couldn't find us at the office.
>
> We had **been** to the cinema three times that week, so we didn't want to go again.

Guidelines

- **has / have gone** means that someone went somewhere and is still there now.
- **has / have been** means that someone went somewhere and then returned back to their departure place and are still at that place.
- **had gone** means that someone went somewhere and was still then when something else happened.
- **had been** means that someone went somewhere and came back.

Choose the correct form

1. They've gone to China for a year, they **will be back next summer / came back last week**.
2. He has **gone / been** home so he's no longer at the office - he'll probably be playing with his children in the garden.
3. Message on kitchen table: I have **gone / been** to the supermarket, back in 20 minutes.
4. She has **been / gone** to Rome - she'll be there till next week.
5. I've just **been / gone** to the supermarket - it was absolutely crowded and it took me ages.
6. By the time I got to the party, most people had already **been / gone** home.
7. We wanted to go to the cinema but our friends had already **been / gone** the night before.
8. Ah, here you are finally. Where have you **been / gone**? I have been waiting for you for hours.
9. Where has Sam **been / gone**? I can't find him anywhere. Maybe he has **been / gone** to lunch.
10. I have **gone / been** to the bank, so I've got the money I owe you.
11. Have you ever **gone / been** to Japan?
12. I have never **gone / been** to work without my umbrella.

1) will be back next summer 2) gone 3) gone 4) gone 5) been 6) gone 7) been (gone) 8) been 9) gone, gone 10) been 11) been 12) gone

Chapter 13
Can vs May

As you can remember, I have always loved jazz.

As you **may** remember, I have always loved jazz.

May you help me with my suitcases?

Can you help me with my suitcases?

Someone can object if it's not true.

Someone **may** object if it's not true.

The woman in the picture can be a manager.

The woman in the picture **may / could** be a manager.

It may be that they have lost our address.

They **may have lost** our address.

He can be in his late 20s.

He **is probably** in his late 20s.

I can say that it was very expensive.

It was very expensive.

© Springer International Publishing AG 2018
A. Wallwork, *Top 50 Grammar Mistakes*, Easy English!,
https://doi.org/10.1007/978-3-319-70984-0_13

> I **can** come next Wednesday at 12 o'clock - so note that down in your diary.
>
> He **may** come next week, but he's not sure at the moment.
>
> (Friend to another friend) **Can** you help me with my homework?
>
> (Shop assistant to customer) **May** I help you? Do you need some assistance?

Guidelines

- Use **can** to express a general ability to do something whenever you want. Examples: *I can play golf. In England it can rain a lot during the summer.*
- Use **can** to express certain 100% possibility, *may* for speculations. Examples: *I can come tomorrow.* (I am certain that I am able to come). *I may come to the meeting.* (Perhaps I will come)
- Use **can** I? (or *may I* - formal) when you want permission. Examples: *Can I (May I) open the window?*
- Use **can you?** in a request: *Can you help me do the washing?*
- Use **may I?** in a formal situation to ask someone if they need assistance: (Shop assistant to client: *May I help you?*)

Choose the correct form

1. **Can / May** I ask you to do me a favor?
2. Let me know if there is anything else I **can / may** do for you.
3. **Can / May** you spell that for me?
4. I **can / may** be late for the meeting, if I am please start without me.
5. **Can / May** I introduce myself? My name is ...
6. I think there **can / may** have been a mistake in my bill - I didn't have anything from the mini bar.
7. I think you **can / may** have misunderstood what Anna said. What she meant was ...
8. Let's arrange a call so that we **can / may** discuss it further.
9. She **can / may** speak five different languages - she's a genius.
10. You **can / may** recall that we met at a party in Sacramento earlier this year.

1) can 2) can 3) can 4) may 5) may (can) 6) may 7) may 8) can 9) can 10) may

Chapter 14
Cannot vs *May Not*

I can not to see very well.

I **cannot see** very well.

They can be annoying for me but cannot be for you.

They **may** be annoying for me but **may not** necessarily be for you.

She said she was rather busy, so she said she cannot come to the party, but let's hope she does.

She said she was rather busy, so she **may not** come to the party, but let's hope she does.

It can be that I don't have enough money to pay the bill.

I **may not** have enough money to pay the bill.

I may not come to the party - I am afraid I will be away that weekend.

I **cannot** come to the party - I am afraid I will be away that weekend

© Springer International Publishing AG 2018
A. Wallwork, *Top 50 Grammar Mistakes*, Easy English!,
https://doi.org/10.1007/978-3-319-70984-0_14

I **cannot** come to the lesson tomorrow because I am on holiday. = It is impossible for me to come.

I **may not** come to the lesson – I will let you know later today if I can or not. = Perhaps I will not come.

She **cannot** be at home yet, she doesn't stop work until after 6 pm.

I would try ringing her later because she **may not** be at home yet.

Guidelines

- **cannot** is generally written as one word, or in the contracted form: **can't.**
  Example: *She can't / cannot speak English very well.*
- Use **cannot** to express 100% impossibility and **may not** for speculations.
  Example: *She cannot come to the meeting.* (It is impossible for her to come).
  I may not be able to come. ((Perhaps I will not come)

Choose the correct form

1. I'm sorry but I **cannot / may not** have enough time to finish doing the painting today.
2. I **cannot / may not** stress how important this is for me.
3. I am sorry but I **cannot / may not** come to your party next week - I have to go away for a business meeting.
4. I think the wifi **cannot / may not** be working correctly - my connection keeps coming and going.
5. At work we **cannot / may not** eat at our desks - it's forbidden.
6. She **cannot / may not** look very intelligent but I can guarantee that she is a genius.
7. I **cannot / may not** be in time for dinner tonight - I will let you know later this evening.
8. It **cannot / may not** have been her that you saw at the supermarket, she's in Brazil at the moment.

1) may not 2) cannot 3) cannot 4) may not 5) cannot 6) may not 7) may not 8) cannot

Chapter 15
Collective Nouns

Manchester United is playing Real Madrid tonight.

Manchester United **are** playing Real Madrid tonight.

The police is investigating the case.

The police **are** investigating the case.

None of the books is worth reading.

None of the books **are** worth reading.

The staff is having a meeting at the moment.

The staff **are** having a meeting at the moment.

The gang is fighting each other.

The gang **are** fighting each other.

© Springer International Publishing AG 2018
A. Wallwork, *Top 50 Grammar Mistakes*, Easy English!,
https://doi.org/10.1007/978-3-319-70984-0_15

> **Most of the companies** in the survey **have** an intranet.
>
> England **has** a population of 54 million.
>
> England **are playing** South Korea in the world cup semi finals.
>
> None of the films I saw **were [was]** any good.
>
> None of the information **was** up to date.
>
> The crew / team / staff / choir **are** all from Mexico.

Guidelines

- When groups of people are viewed in an official manner as a single unit, then the noun is followed by a singular verb (*China is hosting the World Cup*), but when these people are seen as a group of individuals (e.g. a football team) then the noun is followed by a plural verb (*China are playing Russia in the final*).
- Some nouns, such as *crew, team, staff, gang, orchestra* are generally (but not always) followed by a plural verb given that they are seen as individual people rather than as just one single unit.
- Although *none* means *not one*, the verb tends to agree with the main noun (e.g. *none of the artists, none of the speakers, none of the children*) and is thus plural (e.g. *none of the class speak English*).
- If a noun is used with a plural verb then logically the related pronoun will be plural too e.g. *Barcelona are playing at home tonight, they should win*.

Choose the correct form

1. The staff **is / are** always busy so it is difficult to get **its / their** attention.
2. Nike **has / have** announced a new product line.
3. Manchester United **is / are** one of the richest clubs in the world. Tonight **it is / they are** playing in the Champions League.
4. Radiohead **is / are** one of my favorite rock bands. Tonight **it is / they are** playing live at the festival.
5. Our class **is / are** going on a school trip next week.
6. The police **is / are** corrupt. **It / They** often take bribes.
7. The jury **is / are** expected to reach a verdict tonight, when **it / they** will say whether **it thinks / they think** the suspect is guilty of murder or not.
8. The English **are / is** a patriotic and often insular race which explains why **it / they** wanted to leave the European Union.

1) are, their 2) has / have (both are equally possible) 3) is [are], they are 4) is / are, they are 5) is [are] 6) are, they 7) is / are, they, they think 8) are, they

Chapter 16
Comparisons

She is the better in the class.

She is the **best** in the class.

I am worst than you at English.

I am **worse** than you at English.

It was the more expensive I could find.

It was the **most** expensive I could find.

This exercise is more easy than that one.

This exercise is **easier** than that one.

The new reservoir holds ten times water as much as the old one.

The new reservoir holds ten times **as much water** as the old one.

Bigger the mistake more you learn.

The bigger the mistake **the more** you learn.

Her mother is a taller woman.

Her mother is **quite tall.**

They came as late as midnight.

They came **at** midnight.

© Springer International Publishing AG 2018
A. Wallwork, *Top 50 Grammar Mistakes*, Easy English!,
https://doi.org/10.1007/978-3-319-70984-0_16

Microsoft is **bigger than** Amazon.

FIAT is one of the **biggest** companies in Italy.

Mexico City has the second **largest** population in the world.

She is by far the **most** productive person in the company.

Thailand's inflation rate is **not as low as** Japan's.

She doesn't have **as much time as** I do. (OR She has **less** time than me).

They have **as many clients as** us. (**OR the same** number of clients **as** us).

The more I see, **the less** I understand you.

The sooner you send it to me, **the better** (it would be).

Guidelines

- Many adjectives form their comparison and superlative with **more** and **most**. Examples: *more intelligent, the most useful, more polite, the most common*
- Exceptions to the rule above are all adjectives of one syllable, and adjectives that end in *–y* or *–ow*. Examples: *easy > easier, easiest; happy > happier, happiest; narrow > narrower, narrowest*
- There are some irregular adjectives: *good, better, the best; bad, worse, the worst; little, less, the least; much, more, the most; far; further / farther; the furthest / farthest*
- To compare two people, things or events you can use a comparative adjective + than, or a noun + than: *A Ferrari is more expensive than a Fiat.*
- To show that there is no difference between people, things or events use *as* + adjective / noun + *as*. If there is a difference use *as* + adjective / noun + *as*: *Britain's GDP is as big as Italy's GDP.*

Underline the correct form

1. This is the **better / best** party I have ever been to.
2. This is the **more / most** beautiful building in the street.
3. Parties are more popular **than / that** lessons.
4. The weather in England is **worse / worst** than in Mexico.
5. These are the **most easy / easiest** exercises to do.
6. I earn **lesser / less** than she does.
7. London is one of the **more / most** expensive cities in the world.
8. The **longer / more long** it takes the better **it is / is it**.
9. The more **intelligent you are / you are intelligent** the **more / most** difficult life is.
10. They work twice as hard **as / than** I do.
11. This is as big **as / like** that one.
12. This is **as big as / big like** yours.

1) best 2) most 3) than 4) worse 5) easiest 6) less 7) most 8) longer, it is 9) intelligent you are, more 10) as 11) as 12) as big as

Chapter 17
Conditionals: Zero and First (*If* vs *When*)

If I see her, I tell her what you said.

If I see her, I **will** tell her what you said.

You will not pass the exam if you will not study.

You will not pass the exam if you **do** not study.

When you arrive late to a Keith Jarrett concert they don't let you in.

If you arrive late to a Keith Jarrett concert they don't let you in.

I will call the police when she is not back within the next hour.

I will call the police **if** she is not back within the next hour.

When I decide to go to New York this year, I will certainly come and see you.

If I decide to go to New York this year, I will certainly come and see you.

© Springer International Publishing AG 2018
A. Wallwork, *Top 50 Grammar Mistakes*, Easy English!,
https://doi.org/10.1007/978-3-319-70984-0_17

42

> If you **mix** red and green you **get** brown.
>
> If you **arrive** late at my company no one **says** anything - it's all very easy going.
>
> If I **arrive** late tomorrow my boss **will be** very angry - we have a meeting early in the morning.
>
> I **won't pass** the exam if I **don't study**.
>
> **When** I see her, I will tell her. It will either be Monday or Tuesday next week.
>
> **If** I see her, I will tell her. But to be honest I don't see her very often so I can't guarantee anything.

Guidelines

- **if + present + present** (situations that never change, laws). Example: *If you heat ice, it melts.* In this case you could replace *if* with *when* with little difference in meaning. This form is known as the zero conditional.
- **if + present + will** (real hypothesis regarding now or the future). Examples: *If it rains this weekend I will stay at home.* This form is known as the first conditional.
- You can generally switch the two parts of the phrases around. Example: *If you come to the party I will be happy = I will be happy if you come to the party.*
- **when** is always used to introduce a real situation, not a hypothetical situation. *will* means that the speaker thinks / assumes that something will certainly happen at some point (*When I get home, I will call you immediately*). In the example, I may not be sure exactly what time I will arrive home, but I know for sure that I am going home.
- **if** introduces a possibility (*If I get home before midnight, then I will call you, if not, I'll call you tomorrow morning*). In this example, I may or may not arrive home before midnight.
- With the zero conditional (i.e. when making generalizations where the outcome is definite), there may be little difference in meaning between **when** and **if** e.g. *Plants die if / when you don't give them sufficient water.*

Choose the correct form

1. I **tell / will tell** her **if / when** I **see / will see** her at the lesson - she messaged me that she was definitely coming.
2. **Will / Do** let me know if you **hear / will hear** from her? Thanks.
3. If you **press / will press** too hard, it **breaks / will break**.
4. **If / When** I don't go to my English lesson today I **miss / will miss** the test.
5. I **finish / will finish** the report today if I **have / will have** time.
6. My mother will be calling round at some point soon. **When / If** she arrives, just tell her I have popped out to the supermarket.
7. My mother might come round later. **When / If** she does come, just tell her I have popped out to the supermarket.
8. **If / When** I am in Paris next week, I am going to go to the Louvre. I've already booked my ticket.
9. Your plants **die / will die** if you **don't / will not** give them sufficient water.
10. I **don't / won't** generally sleep well if I **drink / will drink** coffee before going to bed.
11. **When / If** you want to go out tonight **you have / you'll have** to clear up first.
12. **When / If** the fire looks as if it is going out, put some more wood on it.

1) will tell, when, see 2) will, hear 3) press, will break (breaks) 4) If I don't go, will miss 5) will finish, have 6) when 7) if 8) when 9) will die, don't 10) don't, drink 11) if 12) if

Chapter 18
Conditionals: Second and Third

If my parents would give me the money I would go on holiday.

If my parents **gave** me the money I would go on holiday.

We would have arrived much earlier if we would not have got lost.

We would have arrived much earlier if we **had not got lost**.

If I had not got married so young it was better.

If I had not got married so young it **would have been** better.

If I would live in the country, I would be happy.

If I **lived** in the country, I would be happy.

I would die, if he had seen me like that.

I **would have died**, if he had seen me like that.

© Springer International Publishing AG 2018   45
A. Wallwork, *Top 50 Grammar Mistakes*, Easy English!,
https://doi.org/10.1007/978-3-319-70984-0_18

> If I **knew** the answer I **would** tell you. But unfortunately I don't know the answer.
>
> I **would study** more if I **had** time. I have so many other things to do which take up all my time.
>
> I **would have traveled** more when I was younger if I **had had** the money, but in reality I was a poor student!
>
> If I **had passed** the exam I **would have been** very happy, but unfortunately I failed.

Guidelines

- **second conditional**: **if + past + *would*** (for 'unreal' hypotheses regarding the present). Example: I *would buy* a house if I *won* the lottery.
- **third conditional**: **if + past perfect + *would have* + past participle** (hypotheses regarding the past). Example: If I *had studied* harder when I was at university I *would have made* my parents happy.
- You can generally switch the two parts of the phrases around. Example: *If you had come earlier it would have been better = It would have been better if you had come earlier.*

Choose the correct form

1. I **worked / would** work in London if I **had / would have** the chance.
2. I'm really sorry. I **would tell / would have told** you earlier if I **had / had had** the chance, but I've been busy all day.
3. If I **am / were** CEO I **will / would** give everyone a raise.
4. If I **were / had been** in charge of the last project I **would delegate / would have delegated** a little more than the project manager did.
5. She seems a bit reluctant to do the presentation. Perhaps if we **gave / had given** her some help with the slides, she **would accept / would have accepted**.
6. It **was / would have been** better if I **had / would** have never met him.
7. I **helped / would help** you if I **had / would have** the time.
8. We ran out of time at the meeting. If we **had / had had** more time, we **would cover / would have covered** all the items on the agenda.

1) would, had 2) would have told, had had 3) were, would 4) had been, would have delegated 5) gave, would accept 6) would have been, had 7) would help, had 8) had had, would have covered

Chapter 19
Continuous Forms

He is thinking that politics is a waste of time.

He **thinks** that politics is a waste of time.

The dog is smelling. She needs a wash.

The dog **smells**. She needs a wash.

She's talked on the phone all morning - when is she going to stop?

She's been talking on the phone all morning - when is she going to stop?

Last weekend I didn't do anything because my girlfriend worked.

Last weekend I didn't do anything because my girlfriend **was working**.

We went for a walk but after an hour it was raining.

We went for a walk but after an hour it **started to rain / it rained**.

© Springer International Publishing AG 2018
A. Wallwork, *Top 50 Grammar Mistakes*, Easy English!,
https://doi.org/10.1007/978-3-319-70984-0_19

48

He **has** two dogs. = He owns / possesses two dogs.

He **is having** lunch with her today. = He has made a future arrangement to eat with her.

They asked me what I **do / did**. = They wanted to know what my job is / was.

They asked me what I **was doing** there. = They wanted to know why I was there at that particular moment.

As I **was telling** you ... = I didn't finish what I wanted to tell you.

As I **told** you ... = I finished what I wanted to tell you but now I want to refer to it again.

He's been talking on the phone all morning. (He is still talking now).

I've talked to her and we've resolved the matter. (I am not talking to her now)

I have been doing my homework that's why I am so tired. Mother: But have you finished it?

I have done my homework so can I play now? Mother: That's great, of course you can.

Guidelines

- Some types of verb are not generally used in the continuous form. They describe states (situations which don't change) rather than actions (things which change): *believe, forget, imagine, know, mean, notice, recognize, remember, think (i.e. have an opinion), understand.* Also verbs that are used to express senses and perception: *feel, hear, see, seem, look, smell, taste.* However some of these verbs can be used in the continuous form, but with a different meaning e.g. *I see (understand) what you mean* vs *I am seeing her tomorrow* (I have an appointment). *What do you think?* (What is your opinion?) *What are you thinking about?* (what's going on in your head?)
- Continuous forms are used to talk about i) an incomplete action: *I have been writing emails all morning, but I haven't finished yet*; ii) a temporary situation that is going on at this moment or was going on at a particularly moment in the past. Examples: *You are reading an explanation of the present continuous. I usually worked in my own office, but on that occasion I was working in Carol's office.*
- The present continuous is also used to talk about future arrangements. Examples: *I am going there tomorrow. She is seeing him tonight.*
- The present perfect continuous is also used to give an explanation for a present situation. Example: *Why are you covered in ink? I've been repairing the photocopier.*

Choose the correct form

1. He **is seeing / sees** her regularly. Next week I **think / am** thinking that he **is seeing / sees** her next week at the festival,
2. It **is smelling / smells** strange, should we take it back?
3. The dog **is smelling / smells** the food - I wonder if he will eat it or not.
4. At the moment, he **is looking / looks** at his notebook.
5. I **lived / was living** in London for ten years before I **came / was coming** here.
6. While I **lived / was living** in London, I **met / was meeting** my wife.
7. I have **written / been writing** emails all morning – I have **written / been writing** 20 so far.
8. He **has worked / been working** too hard that's why he's always so tired.
9. He **has worked / been working** for several different companies. He **has worked / been working** for his current company for six months.
10. She **has read / has been reading** that book before and she doesn't want to read it again.

1) sees, think, is seeing 2) smells 3) is smelling 4) is looking 5) lived, came 6) was living, met 7) been writing, written 8) been working 9) has worked, been working 10) has read

Chapter 20
Countable and Uncountable Nouns

Excuse me, is there a news for me?

Excuse me, is there **any news** for me?

The news about her aunt are not good.

The news about her aunt **is** not good.

He has such a bad taste.

He has **such bad** taste.

He's losing his hairs with all this stress.

He's losing **his hair** with all this stress.

I asked a staff at the informations desk.

I asked **a staff member** at the **information** desk.

I have a lot of experiences in writing reports.

I have a lot of **experience** in writing reports.

Look at the damages she has done to our car.

Look at the **damage** she has done to our car.

They have done many researches on this.

They have done **a lot of research** on this.

This may be an evidence against astrology.

This may be **evidence** against astrology.

We went to the mall, had a lunch, and then saw a movie.

We went to the mall, had **lunch**, and then saw a movie.

© Springer International Publishing AG 2018
A. Wallwork, *Top 50 Grammar Mistakes*, Easy English!,
https://doi.org/10.1007/978-3-319-70984-0_20

The most important **feedback is** the **feedback** you get day by day.

Can you give me **some feedback** on this doc? Can you tell me what you think about this doc?

I needed **some furniture** - I needed a bed and a wardrobe.

IKEA **furniture is** very cheap.

She's doing **a training course**. She's doing **some training.**

Paper is becoming an expensive commodity.

She reads **the paper** (i.e. a newspaper) every day.

Guidelines

- Countable nouns are things we can count. They can be made plural using an 's' and can be preceded by **a / an / one**. Examples: *A book, one book, two books; a plan, one plan, several plans*
- Uncountable nouns are things we cannot count. They cannot be made plural using an 's' and cannot be preceded by **a / an / one**. They are often materials, liquids and abstract things. Examples: *water, gold, health, baggage, proof, help*
- Some words may be uncountable in English but countable in other languages. Examples: *accommodation, advertising, advice, progress, traffic, work*
- To express a quantity using an uncountable noun, you need to use particular words and expressions. Examples: *Can you give me **some** feedback on my proposal? They're earning **a great deal of** money.*
- In some cases (e.g. *business, experience, glass, paper*) nouns can be both countable or uncountable depending on their use. Example: *Is there any wine left? This shop sells wines from Spain and Italy.*

The following sentences contain mistakes regarding uncountable nouns that have mistakenly been used as if they were countable. Identify the mistakes and correct them

1. There are evidences that she stole the money.
2. I owe you ten dollars, I will give you them on Monday.
3. There are few knowledge about the best way to do this.
4. This causes many traffics on the network.
5. They are doing a research into rats.
6. We have made a progress.
7. We used a software in our calculations.
8. She had a good luck and won the prize.
9. He was playing a loud music.
10. It was such a bad weather that we had to go home.

KEY

1. There **is evidence** that she stole the money.
2. I owe you ten dollars, I will give you **it** on Monday.
3. There **is little knowledge** about the best way to do this.
4. This causes **a lot of traffic** on the network.
5. They are doing **some research** into rats.
6. We have made **(some) progress**.
7. We used **a software application** in our calculations.
8. She had **good luck** and won the prize.
9. He was playing **loud music**.
10. It was **such bad weather** that we had to go home.

Chapter 21
Each, Every, All, None

Almost each family has a fiber optic connection now.

Almost **every** family has a fiber optic connection now.

Each of the students were afraid.

All of the students were afraid.

All of the students were not afraid.

None of the students **were** afraid.

Each of us did not have an umbrella.

None of us had an umbrella.

Everyone are happy with the pay rise.

Everyone **is** happy with the pay rise.

The prices are low for every goods.

The prices are low for **all the** goods.

These oranges are $1 for each.

These oranges are $1 **each**.

© Springer International Publishing AG 2018
A. Wallwork, *Top 50 Grammar Mistakes*, Easy English!,
https://doi.org/10.1007/978-3-319-70984-0_21

Each correct answer is worth 10 points.

I know the name of **every** student in the school.

I could hear **every** word they said.

The train runs **every** three minutes.

None of the books is / are worth reading.

Everyone of us had been there before. We had **all** been there before.

Guidelines

- **each** + singular noun – focus on the individual rather than the group (e.g. *The teacher gives each student individual attention.*)
- **every** + singular noun – focus more on the group as a whole (e.g. *Every student has to attend every course.*) However, *every* can also be used when the stress is on the individual.
- **all** + uncountable noun or plural countable noun (e.g. *I will give you all the information and all the books you need.*)
- **every** and **all** are not generally used with *not*. This means that instead of saying: ~~All the students / Every student did not pass the exam~~ You should say: *None of the students passed the exam.* Or alternatively: *All the students / Every student failed the exam.*

Choose the correct form

1. At **each / every / all** age, girls and women face **each / every / all** other directly when sitting on public transport.
2. On the other hand, boys and men sit at angles to **each / every / all** other and so that they don't have to look at **each / every / all** other..
3. Data are refreshed **each / every / all** minute.
4. **None of us could / Every one of us could not** get to sleep.
5. Italian is a phonetic language in which **each / every / all** letters are pronounced distinctly - this means it is possible to pronounce **each / every / all** word in the language without having previously heard it.
6. In Japanese **each / every / all** syllable has the same length and strength.
7. In English nearly **each / every / all** word seem to follow their own rules.
8. The system automatically sends an email **each / every / all** third Thursday.
9. **Each / Every / All** mails that bounce back are then removed from the list of recipients.
10. **All / None / Each** of them could come to the party - so in the end the party was cancelled.

1) every, each 2) each, each 3) every 4) none of us could 5) all letters, every 6) each / every 7) all) 8) every 9) all 10) none

Chapter 22
Few, Little, A Few, A Little

Few days ago I met him at the station.

A few days ago I met him at the station.

With the few money they gave me I was unable to buy fresh food.

With the **little** money they gave me I was unable to buy fresh food.

He knows a little about this subject, almost nothing in fact.

He knows **little** about this subject, almost nothing in fact.

Little people have seen this film.

Few people have seen this film.

We only have a few informations on this.

We only have **a little information** on this.

© Springer International Publishing AG 2018
A. Wallwork, *Top 50 Grammar Mistakes*, Easy English!,
https://doi.org/10.1007/978-3-319-70984-0_22

60

> **Few** people know this. = Hardly anyone / Almost no one knows about this.
>
> **A few** people know this. = Some people know this, but not many.
>
> **Little** has been done to help the poor. = Not enough / Very very little has been done.
>
> **A little** has been done to help the poor. = Something has been done, so a minimum amount of progress is being made.

Guidelines

- **a little** and **little** + singular uncountable noun.
- **a few** and **few** + plural noun.
- **a little** means 'something but not (too) much'; **a few** is the plural equivalent of **a little**.
- **little** means 'almost nothing', **few** means 'almost none'. Both **few** and **little** underline a negative situation.

Choose the correct form

1. She sounded **a little / little / a few / few** annoyed when I telephone her.
2. **A few / Few / A little / Little** business people can claim with any justification or credibility that they deserve to earn in one year what the population of an entire town in Africa earns in a decade.
3. Would you like **a little / little / a few / few** more to eat?
4. Do you think you could speak up **a little / little / a few / few**, please?
5. **A few / Few / A little / Little** is known about the real nature of ghosts, though **a few / few / a little / little** people claim to have seen them.
6. Have you got **a little / little / a few / few** minutes? I have **a little / little / a few / few** questions I would like to ask you.
7. I have made **a little / little / a few / few** changes to our plans, I hope that is OK with you, in any case **a little / little / a few / few** has changed in terms of the main ideas.

1) a little 2) few 3) a little 4) a little 5) little, a few 6) a few, a few 7) a few, little

Chapter 23
(This Is The) First Time, Second Time

This is only the second time I try Chinese food.

This is the only the second time I **have tried** Chinese food.

This is the first time we are all together.

This is the first time we **have all been** together.

This is the first time I am taking a language course.

This is the first time I **have taken** a language course.

It was the first time I traveled by plane.

It was the first time I **had traveled** by plane.

Is this the first time you come here?

Is this the first time you **have come / been** here?

© Springer International Publishing AG 2018
A. Wallwork, *Top 50 Grammar Mistakes*, Easy English!,
https://doi.org/10.1007/978-3-319-70984-0_23

> It **is** the first time that I **have worked** like this. = I have never worked like this before.
>
> This **is** the third time that I **have told** you this rule. = I have told you this rule three times before.
>
> This **is** not the first time that I **have come** here. = I have been here before.
>
> It **was** the first time that I **had worked** like that. = I had never worked so much in all my life.

Guidelines

- **this is the first / second / third etc time that** + present perfect (*has / have* + past participle). The present perfect is used because the sentence means *From the day I was born up until the present day, I have never done a certain thing* i.e. there is a connection between a point in the past (*the day I was born*) until the present time (i.e. today, the moment I am speaking).
- **it was the first / second / third etc time that** + past perfect (*had* + past participle). The past perfect is used because the sentence means *From one particular moment in the past until another particular moment in the past, I had never done a certain thing*.

Complete the second phrase so that it means the same as the first phrase

1. This is the first time that I have heard this music. = I have _____
2. I have never done a presentation before. = This is the first time _____
3. It was the first time she had seen the film. = She _____
4. From the day I was born I this is only the second time I have come here. = I have _____
5. They had never seen an elephant before. = That was the first time _____
6. This is the first time I have understood this rule. = I _____

1. I have never heard this music before.
2. This is the first time I have done a presentation.
3. She had never seen the film before.
4. I have only come / been here once before.
5. That was the first time they had seen an elephant.
6. I have never understood this rule before.

Chapter 24
Genitive: The Possessive Form of Nouns

This is the John's book.

This is **John's** book.

The lesson of Tuesday is canceled.

Tuesday's lesson is canceled.

The Trump's administration made many mistakes.

The **Trump** administration made many mistakes.

This is a typical everyday's problem.

This is a typical **everyday** problem.

This is an Alfred Hitchcock's movie.

This is an **Alfred Hitchcock** movie.

I read a Harry Potter's book.

I read a Harry **Potter book** / I read one of the books **about Harry Potter**.

© Springer International Publishing AG 2018
A. Wallwork, *Top 50 Grammar Mistakes*, Easy English!,
https://doi.org/10.1007/978-3-319-70984-0_24

My wife writes **history books**. She is writing a book on **the history of England**.

Look at this bookshelf. The books on the left are my books (i.e. books that I have bought) and those on the right are my **wife's** (i.e. books that she has bought).

My **sister's** husband is not coming to **tomorrow's** party.

I have many friends. I went to my **friends'** party (i.e. **Jack and Jill's** party) last night. The night before I went to my **friend's** house (i.e. **Pete's** house).

Guidelines

- The genitive (possessive form) is formed by adding 's after a singular noun, or simply an apostrophe (') after a plural noun or a noun that already ends in s (NB s's is also possible).
- The genitive indicates that something belongs to someone, to some group of people or to some animal e.g. *John's book* (this generally means that the book was bought by John and thus belongs to John).
- When we are talking about the author of a book or the director of a movie, often the genitive is not used. Compare *I read a good Stephen King book* vs *Stephen King's new book is called xxx. I like Woody Allen movies* vs *Woody Allen's last movie was called xxx.*
- The genitive can also be used in certain expressions of time and distance e.g. *I am going a three weeks' time. It's a minute's walk from here.*
- The genitive is not normally used with animate objects.

Choose the correct form

1. How do you measure **a circle's area / the area of a circle**?
2. I have a **software's / software** problem.
3. I studied at **Cambridge's / Cambridge** University.
4. She has an **Apple / Apple's** iPhone 12.
5. My **professor's / professor** lessons are really boring.
6. It is **mile's / mile** walk from here.
7. My two **sisters' / sister's / sister** children are coming today.
8. I am watching a *Game of* **Thrones / Thrones'** episode.
9. This is **the Helen's / Helen's / Helen** car.

1) the area of a circle 2) software 3) Cambridge (or: the University of Cambridge) 4) Apple 5) professor's 6) mile's 7) sisters' 8) Thrones 9) Helen's

Chapter 25
Have, Have Got

Have you got a dog? Yes I've.

Have you got a dog? Yes I **have**.

Do you have time? Yes, I have got.

Do you have time? Yes, I do / Yes, I have.

Hypochondria is the one disease I don't have got.

Hypochondria is the one disease **I don't have**.

I've a meeting in 10 minutes, have you got one too?

I have a meeting in 10 minutes, **do you have** one too?

After buying the house, they had not very much money left.

After buying the house, **they did not have** very much money left.

© Springer International Publishing AG 2018
A. Wallwork, *Top 50 Grammar Mistakes*, Easy English!,
https://doi.org/10.1007/978-3-319-70984-0_25

> **Do you have** time for a drink? Yes, I **do**. Sorry I **don't**.
>
> **We're having** a party tomorrow.
>
> She **has / She's got** two cars.
>
> **Did you have** a good holiday? Yes, I **did**. No, I **didn't**.
>
> I'm sorry I **didn't have** time to do the exercise.

Guidelines

- **to have** generally functions as a normal verb and so uses *do* and *does* as its auxiliaries. Contracted forms (*I've, we've* etc) are usually followed by **got**, which indicates possession only.
- **got** is only required to indicate possession, but is not necessary (*I've got a car = I have a car*). **got** cannot be used to indicate habits and activities such as *I have got a shower every morning*.
- the contracted forms *I've, she's, they've* must be just with **got** to indicate possession (*she's got a dog*, not: *she's a dog*), otherwise the full form should be used (*she has a dog*).
- **got** is not generally used in the past. The past is *had* (+), *didn't have* (-), *did you have* (?), just like any other verb. Examples: *I had a dog. I didn't have a dog. Did you have a dog?*
- In short answers, never use the contracted forms. *Have got a car? Yes, I have* (Not: *Yes, I've*).

Choose the correct form

1. **She's / She's got** a horse.
2. **He has / He's** lunch in his taxi.
3. **They've / they've got** a lot of time on their hands.
4. **I've / I've got** many gadgets for sale if you're interested.
5. **Have you / Do you have** a car?
6. I **hadn't / didn't have** many trips to do last year.
7. **Have you / Do you have** anything to drink?
8. We are **having / having got** a party, do you want to come?
9. I don't generally **have / have got** breakfast, I just go to a bar mid morning.
10. Do **you have / you've** your cell phone with you? Yes **I've / I do**.

1) she's got 2) he has 3) they've got 4) I've got 5) do you have 6) didn't have 7) do you have 8) having 9) have 10) you have, do

Chapter 26
Have Something Done

I am not going to make cut my hair by my mum.

I am not going to **have my hair cut** by my mum.

She is having her house to paint next week.

She is having her house **painted** next week.

Do you make clean your house by an outside service?

Do you **have your house cleaned** by an outside service?

I am having done my nails tomorrow.

I am having **my nails done** tomorrow.

I am getting a lifting to my face.

I am **going to get a facelift**.

© Springer International Publishing AG 2018
A. Wallwork, *Top 50 Grammar Mistakes*, Easy English!,
https://doi.org/10.1007/978-3-319-70984-0_26

> They **are having** their house **renovated**.
>
> I **had** / I **got** my hair **cut** yesterday.
>
> We are **having** someone **paint** the living room for us.
>
> She **is having** her tonsils **removed**.
>
> I finally **got her to tell** the truth.

Guidelines

- **to have / get something done** (*have / get* + service + past participle) means to have a service carried out for you by someone else
- **to have someone do something** (have + person + infinitive + service) is another way of saying *to have something done*
- **to get someone to do** something means the same as *to have someone do something*, but note that *to get* requires the infinitive with *to*
- don't confuse *to have someone do something* with *to make someone do something*. to **make** means to *force / oblige*. Thus, *I made him clean the house* means that I forced him to clean the house against probably against his will

Choose the correct form

1. She is having an online service **to write / write** an essay for her.
2. She's **getting / letting** someone **do / to do** the gardening for her - she's so lazy.
3. I am having my car **to fix / fixed** next week.
4. She is having **dyed her hair / her hair dyed** at the hairdresser's.
5. The company are **having built / building** a new office.
6. They are having the office **built / building** by a construction company.
7. They get all their printing **to do / done** externally.
8. I'll **get / have** my secretary do the photocopies.
9. I'll **get / have** my husband to give you a call.
10. Are you doing the painting yourself or are you having **done the painting / the painting done** for you?

1) write 2)) getting, to do 3) fixed 4) her hair dyed 6) building 7) built 8) have 9) have 10) the painting done

Chapter 27
How Long, How Much Time, How Many Times

How long time do you live here?

How **long have you been living** here?

From how much time have you been working for yourself?

How long have you been working for yourself?

How much time have you seen this movie?

How many times have you seen this movie?

How time do we have to do this exercise?

How much time do we have to do this exercise?

Who knows how long she is crying.

Who knows how long she **has been** crying.

© Springer International Publishing AG 2018
A. Wallwork, *Top 50 Grammar Mistakes*, Easy English!,
https://doi.org/10.1007/978-3-319-70984-0_27

> **How long** have you been living in London?
>
> **How long** will you be staying here?
>
> **How many times** have you been to New York? I have been to New York six times.
>
> **How much time** do we have available? Just a couple of hours.

Guidelines

- Use **how long** to find out the duration of a particular activity. Note: **how long** is found with the **PRESENT PERFECT (CONTINUOUS)** when it refers to an action that began in the past and is still true today. Example: *How long have you been studying / have you studied English?* (implies that you are still studying English now). When used with the simple past, **how long** refers to a completed action. Example: *How long did your first marriage last?* (implies that your first marriage is over / finished).
- **how long** can also be used with reference to the future. In any case, the form ~~how long time~~ does not exist.
- **how many times** is used to find out the number of times someone has done a particular activity. Note the concordance in the use of the plural forms - *many* + *-s* (times).
- the word *time* in **how much time**, refers to minutes, hours, days, etc.

Choose the correct form

1. How **time / much time** are you planning to stay here?
2. How **many times / much time** do you have to ring the bell before they answer?
3. How long **do you work / have you been working** here?
4. How **long time / long** are you here for? I am leaving the day after tomorrow.
5. How **many times / much time** do you think it will take to complete this exercise?
6. How **many times / much time** do you think you will need to practise this piece before you can do it perfectly?

1) much time 2) many times 3) have you been working 4) long 5) much time 6) both forms are possible

Chapter 28
-ing Form vs the Infinitive

To cook is a very enjoyable activity.

Cooking is a very enjoyable activity.

After to teach you I will go home.

After **teaching** you I will go home.

I look forward to hear from you.

I look forward to **hearing** from you.

While to watch the film I fell asleep.

While **watching** the film I fell asleep.

How long will it take for reaching the next town?

How long will it take **to reach** the next town?

© Springer International Publishing AG 2018
A. Wallwork, *Top 50 Grammar Mistakes*, Easy English!,
https://doi.org/10.1007/978-3-319-70984-0_28

To have a good memory you **need to do** a specialized course.

Having a good memory is really useful.

Before using it you **need to attach** the headphones.

I look forward **to hearing** from you.

We **would like to inform** you that we have **decided to accept** your proposal.

This programme **allows / enables / permits you to write** spreadsheets.

I **persuaded him to let** me use his mobile.

Guidelines

- The **-ing form** focuses on the <u>activity</u> (e.g. *Learning English is easy*). The **infinitive form** focuses on the <u>objective</u> or what you have to do to achieve an objective (e.g. *To learn English you need to study hard*).
- Use the **-ing form** immediately after *before, after, by, about, on, for, in, to* etc.
- Use the **-ing form** after verbs that express: a) ideas, advice, e.g. *recommend, propose, suggest* (see Chapter 1); b) how much we enjoy or enjoyed something, e.g. *like, love, hate, enjoy* (see Chapter 30); c) *-ing* is also used after verbs: *risk, avoid, spend time, mind*.
- Use the **infinitive** a) when you focus on a purpose or objective, e.g. *would like, want, plan, promise, decide, hope*; b) when you tell someone what they can do or what we want them to do: *allow, ask, enable, expect, help, instruct, permit, persuade, tell*.
- Use the **infinitive** generally after adjectives and with *how*. Examples: *It's easy to use. If you like I'll show you how to use one.*

Choose the correct form

1. **Studying / To study** English is more difficult than people think.
2. We are in the process of **reconstruct / reconstructing** our website.
3. Thank you for your help in **solve / solving** this problem.
4. Sorry for the delay in **to get / getting** back to you.
5. **Making / to make** cakes is easy but **making / to make** a cake you need the right ingredients.
6. If you need any further details do not hesitate **to contact / contacting** me.
7. **Playing / To play** football is fun, but **playing / to play** really well you need to train most days a week.
8. I look forward to **do / doing** business with you and showing you how **using / to use** our products.
9. Most Italians enjoy **spending / to spend** time with their family.
10. It's not difficult **learning / to learn** - you will soon get the hang of it.

1) studying 2) reconstructing 3) solving 4) getting 5) making, to make 6) to contact
7) playing / to play 8) doing, to use 9) spending 10) to learn

Chapter 29
Languages and Nationalities

Did you learn the Greek at school?

Did you learn **Greek** at school?

He speaks a good English.

He **speaks good** English.

She doesn't know the English.

She doesn't **speak English**.

The Spanish is simpler than the English.

Spanish is simpler than **English**.

English are a strange race.

The English are a strange race.

I met one English and one Dutch.

I met **an English person** and **a Dutch person**.

I met someone from England and **someone from Holland.**

There were two Japaneses on the train.

There were two **Japanese people / men / women** on the train.

© Springer International Publishing AG 2018
A. Wallwork, *Top 50 Grammar Mistakes*, Easy English!,
https://doi.org/10.1007/978-3-319-70984-0_29

> **English** is a relatively easy language.
>
> For some people, **the English** spoken in the UK is more pure than **the English** spoken in the US.
>
> **The English** are a conservative race.
>
> He comes from Wales, he is **Welsh**, he speaks **Welsh**. **The Welsh** are very patriotic.
>
> I met **an Italian, two Americans, many Albanians** and **several Chinese people.**

Guidelines

- Languages are not countable, this means that you cannot put **a / an** in front of them. Example: *They speak* ~~an~~ *amazing French.*
- Languages do not require **the** unless you are differentiating between varieties of the same language. Example: *The French spoken in Belgium is different from the French spoken in Canada.*
- We generally say *to speak* a language rather than *to know*.
- Nationalities that end in *-ese*, *-ss* and *-h* do not have a plural form. So instead of saying *two* ~~Chineses~~ you have to say *two Chinese people* (or *two Chinese men / women / children* etc). Likewise, although you can say *Italians / Americans love pasta* you cannot say ~~English~~ *love pasta*, instead say *The English / The Swiss / The Portuguese love pasta* or alternatively *English people / Swiss people / Portuguese people love pasta.*

Choose the correct form

1. Her students all speak **a perfect / perfect** English.
2. **Spanish / The Spanish** is quite similar to **the Italian / Italian**.
3. I **know / speak** Japanese quite well.
4. There are several **Chineses / forms of Chinese** - the main one is **the Mandarin / Mandarin**.
5. **The French / French** I learned at school did not help me at all when I first lived in France.
6. In my class there is **a Senegalese / a Senegalese student** who speaks **French / the French**.
7. **The French / French** are quite patriotic and I admire the way they try to promote their culture over American culture.
8. **The Americans / Americans** tend to be quite loud, particularly **the Americans / Americans** that I met in Texas.

1) perfect 2) Spanish, Italian 3) speak 4) forms of Chinese, Mandarin 5) the French 6) a Senegalese student, French 7) the French 8) Americans (the Americans), the Americans (i.e. specific Americans)

Chapter 30
Like, Love, Prefer

Would you like going to the movies with me?

Would you like **to go** to the movies with me?

Do you like me to show you how to do it?

Would you like me to show you how to do it?

She doesn't like when I use a curse word.

She doesn't like **it** when I use a curse word.

They prefer living in the country more than living in a town.

They prefer living in the country **to** living in a town.

I like smoke.

I like **smoking / to smoke**.

If you don't mind I would prefer going to bed.

If you don't mind I would prefer **to go** to bed.

I don't prefer to go now.

I **would prefer not to go** now. I **would rather not go** now.

I don't like that he eats with his mouth open.

I don't like **him eating** with his mouth open.

© Springer International Publishing AG 2018
A. Wallwork, *Top 50 Grammar Mistakes*, Easy English!,
https://doi.org/10.1007/978-3-319-70984-0_30

> I like / liked **playing** tennis. (GB) I like / liked **to play** tennis. (US)
>
> I would like **to play** tennis. (GB and US)
>
> I like to **play** tennis in the morning rather than the afternoon. (habit)
>
> I like **playing** tennis with Tom because I always win. (enjoyment)
>
> I don't like **it** when she beats me at tennis.
>
> I would prefer **to play** with Tom than with Rick.
>
> I would prefer **not to go** alone.
>
> **Wouldn't** you prefer to go out to dinner rather than cooking at home tonight?

Guidelines

- Generally speaking, use the **-ing** form after *like* (and *love*) and *prefer* when these verbs are in the present or past, and the **infinitive** form when they are in the conditional form.
- Do not use the present tense with *like* and *prefer* when you are asking about a present situation rather than a habitual situation e.g. *Would you prefer / like to go now?* rather than *D̶o̶ you prefer / like to go now?*
- After *like* (and *love*) use *it* in expressions such as *I like / love i̲t̲ when he holds my hand*.
- When comparing two items use *I prefer x t̲o̲ y*. Do not use *than* in such cases.
- There is a subtle (but not very important) difference between, for example, *I like* + infinitive and *I like* + ing. The infinitive focuses on my particular habits (i.e. this is what I usually do). The *-ing* form focuses on my enjoyment of the activity.

Choose the correct form

1. I would prefer **going / to go** there later.
2. Why do you prefer jazz **than / to** classical music?
3. I **love / would love** to watch a movie tonight.
4. **Do / Would** you like to come with me?
5. **Do / Would** you generally prefer white or red wine?
6. I **like it / like** when we do listening exercises in class.
7. I love **watching / to watch** sports live - it is so much more fun than watching sports on TV.
8. **Do / Would** you prefer **waiting / to wait**, or do you want to go straightaway?
9. I like **eating / to eat** pizza - it's my favorite food.
10. I like **eating / to eat** pizza with beer rather than wine - this is my preference and I've noticed that Italians prefer **to do / doing** this too.

1) to go 2) to 3) would love 4) would 5) do 6) like it 7) watching 8) would, to wait 9) eating (to eat) 10) to eat, to do

Chapter 31
Make vs *Let*

She let us to leave early.

She let **us leave** early.

They let us to think that they were experts in the field.

They **made us think** that they were experts in the field.

They made us work on our own, which was great because we all like working independently.

They **let** us work on our own, which was great because we all like working independently.

He made me to study all the rules.

He made **me study** all the rules.

Do you make build your house by a construction company?

Are you having your house built by a construction company?

© Springer International Publishing AG 2018   83
A. Wallwork, *Top 50 Grammar Mistakes*, Easy English!,
https://doi.org/10.1007/978-3-319-70984-0_31

The mother **made** her son stay at home. He wanted to go out but she wouldn't let him go.

The mother **let** her son stay at home because he didn't want to go to school.

The teacher **made** the bad student **stay** behind after the lesson.

They **made us work** more than twelve hours a day six days a week.

We **were made to work** twelve hours a day. = They **made** us work.

We **were not allowed to go** home unless we had worked twelve hours = They didn't **let** us go.

Guidelines

- **to make someone do** something means to oblige or force someone to do something, probably against their will.
- **to let someone do something** means to give them permission, to allow them.
- in the active form **to make** and **to let** take the infinitive without *to*. Examples: *They made me to confess and then they let me to go.*
- in the passive form **to make** requires the infinitive with *to*. Example: *I was made to wait five hours before being seen by the doctor.*
- there is no passive form of **to let**, instead **to be allowed** is used. *My teacher let me use a dictionary = I was allowed (by the teacher) to use a dictionary.*
- don't confuse **to make someone do something** with TO HAVE SOMEONE DO SOMETHING. to *make* means to *force / oblige*, whereas *have someone do something* means to get a third party to do a task for you.

Choose the correct form

1. They let us **to go / go** together but made us **to promise / promise** not to talk to each other.
2. We **made / were made** to be together, I don't want to **make / let** anything get in our way.
3. After much insistence on our part, they **let / made** us pay for the meal.
4. The restaurant manager **let / made** us pay for the meal even though we told her it was inedible.
5. They are **making / letting** me **work / to work** overtime despite all my protests.
6. My mother **makes / lets** me do my homework, even if I don't want to do it.
7. Will you **let / make** me **go / to go** please - you're hurting me.
8. She wasn't **let / allowed** to go inside the pub because she was underage.
9. I **let / made** him stay for a week even though it was really inconvenient for me.
10. I **made / got / had** an online service to write my thesis for me.

1) go, promise 2) were made, let 3) let 4) made 5) making, work 6) makes 7) let, go
8) allowed 9) let 10) had

Chapter 32
Much, Many, A Lot of, Lots of

I have much work at the moment.

I have **a lot of** work at the moment.

How much times have you been there?

How **many** times have you been there?

Was there much people?

Were there **many** people?

You don't need many money to do this.

You don't need **much / a lot of** money to do this.

There are many evidences to support this view.

There is **a lot of evidence** to support this view.

There are many softwares to do this.

There are **many software applications / is a lot of software** to do this.

© Springer International Publishing AG 2018
A. Wallwork, *Top 50 Grammar Mistakes*, Easy English!,
https://doi.org/10.1007/978-3-319-70984-0_32

I have **a lot of / lots of / many** friends.

I **don't** have **many (a lot of)** enemies.

I have **a lot of** time.

I **don't** have **much (a lot of)** time.

We have **a lot of** information.

We **do not** have **much** information.

Does he earn **a lot of / lots of / much** money?

Guidelines

- **much** - used with UNCOUNTABLE NOUNS (see Chapter 20), generally in negative and interrogative.
- **many** - used with plural nouns, generally in negative and interrogative.
- **a lot of** - used with all nouns, typically in the affirmative but also in the interrogative.
- **lots of** - can replace *a lot of* in affirmative, but **lots of** is not suitable for formal situations. **lots of** is very rarely used in negative phrases, and is also quite rare in questions.

Choose the correct form(s). Note: read the section on UNCOUNTABLE NOUNS (see Chapter 20), before doing this exercise

1. Are there **a lot of / lots of / many / much** teachers at this school?
2. How **much / many** friends do you have on Facebook?
3. I have **a lot of / lots of / many / much** books on this subject.
4. Do you have **a lot of / lots of / many** students from Africa?
5. We don't have **a lot of / lots of / many** students from Africa.
6. We have **a lot of homework / much homework / many homeworks** to do tonight.
7. We don't have **lots of homework / much homework / many homeworks** to do tonight.
8. There **aren't many options / isn't much option** left I'm afraid.
9. There **aren't many wines / isn't much wine** left in the bottle I'm afraid.
10. This supermarket sells **much wine / many wines** from all over the world.
11. Do you have **much baggage / many baggages** with you? Yes, I have **a lot of / much** suitcases.
12. There is **much / there are many / there are a lot of** staff on duty today.
13. The earthquake created **a lot of damage / much damage / many damages**.
14. I have **a lot of / lots of / much / many** news to tell you.
15. The house doesn't have **much furniture / many furnitures** in it.
16. They did **a lot of training / much training / many trainings** to learn how to be a teacher.
17. We haven't made **lots of progress / much progress / many progresses** so far.
18. She gave me **a lot of advice / much advice / many advices**.
19. Was there **a lot of traffic / much traffic / many traffics** on the road today?
20. How **much feedback / many feedbacks** do you get from your boss?

1) a lot of / many 2) many 3) a lot of / lots of / many 4) many (a lot of) 5) many (a lot of) 6) a lot of homework 7) much homework 8) aren't many option 9) isn't much wine 10) many wines 11) much baggage 12) a lot of 13) a lot of damage 14) a lot of / lots of 15) much furniture 16) a lot of training 17) much progress 18) a lot of advice 19) much (a lot of) 20) much feedback

Chapter 33
Must vs *Have To*

I must change train in Rome - there is no train that goes direct.

I **have to** change train in Rome - there is no train that goes direct.

I must be at work before 10 every morning - although my boss is quite flexible.

I **have to be** [I am supposed to be] at work before 10 every morning - although my boss is quite flexible.

Have you to do it immediately?

Do you have to do it immediately?

I've to go now - sorry.

I **have to** go now - sorry.

At our school we must arrive at 8.0.

At our school we **have to** arrive at 8.0. We **have to** be at school at 8.0.

© Springer International Publishing AG 2018
A. Wallwork, *Top 50 Grammar Mistakes*, Easy English!,
https://doi.org/10.1007/978-3-319-70984-0_33

> *Teacher to young children*: You **must study**.
>
> *Student*: You **have to study** a lot on this course.
>
> *Mother to young child*: You **must eat** your food.
>
> *Child*: My mother says I **have to eat** all my vegetables.
>
> *Police officer to car driver*: You **must wear** a seatbelt at all times.
>
> *English person to foreigner*: In England you **have to wear** a seatbelt.

Guidelines

- **have to** is used to talk about our general responsibilities. Thus, to show that an obligation probably comes from some other person not from us use *have to*. Examples: *Every day I have to catch the train to work. We have to arrive at work before nine. I have to do a lot of work around the house.* In all these cases the speaker receives an obligation from another person or simply explains that the choice does not necessarily depend on them.
- **have to** behaves like a regular verb: *I have to, she has to; Do I have to, Does she have to? I don't have to, She doesn't have to. I had to, She had to; Did you have to, Did she have to; I didn't have to, She didn't have to*
- use the full form of **have**: *I have to* and not ~~I've to~~
- **must** is used much less frequently than to **have to**. It is used when an authority gives a 'subordinate' an order (e.g. police officer to citizen, parent to child) - such situations are rare. It is also used to give a very strong recommendation or when there is a real emergency / urgency. Examples: *You must go and see that movie – you would love it. Doctor, you must come immediately. I really must answer her email otherwise I might lose a great opportunity.*

Underline the most suitable form

1. **Have I / Do I have** to tell him? Yes, you **do / have**.
2. Could you send his email address as I think I **must / have to** got his old one.
3. I know you **must / have to** be very busy but ...
4. I'm sorry, but I'll **must / have to** interrupt you - I **must / have** to take this call.
5. I **must / have to** go to the dentist for regular check ups.
6. Sorry but your email **must / has to** have gone into the spam.
7. We generally **have to / must** be at work before 09.30.
8. You **have to / must** come and see us when you're next in town.
9. Notice: Helmets **must** be worn on the building site at all times.
10. **Do you have to / Must you** clock in when you go to work?

1) do I have, do 2) must 3) must 4) have to, have to 5) have to 6) must 7) have to 8) must 9) must 10) do you have

Chapter 34
Must Not Vs *Do Not Have To*

He was left a lot of money so he hasn't to work.

He was left a lot of money so he **does not have** to work.

We have not to do a written exam, just an oral one.

We **do not have** to do a written exam, just an oral one.

Thank you but you hadn't to go to so much trouble.

Thank you but you **didn't have to** go [you should not have gone] to so much trouble.

You do not have feed the animals.

[Please] **don't feed** the animals.

You have not to smoke in enclosed public spaces.

You **mustn't** smoke in enclosed public spaces.

Haven't we to go now?

Don't we have to go now?

I'd like you to help me with this, but it hasn't to be now.

I'd like you to help me with this, but I **can't** now.

© Springer International Publishing AG 2018
A. Wallwork, *Top 50 Grammar Mistakes*, Easy English!,
https://doi.org/10.1007/978-3-319-70984-0_34

You **don't have to come** if you don't want to. = You don't need to come ...

You **mustn't come** before 6 o'clock or you will ruin the surprise. = I absolutely don't want you to come.

You **mustn't smoke** in a non-smoking compartment. = This is the law.

You **don't have to do** a written exam, just an oral. = There is no written exam.

Guidelines

- **to have to** behaves like a regular verb. So the negative form is *doesn't have to, don't have to, didn't have to*. The forms ~~haven't to~~, ~~haven't to~~ and ~~haven't to~~ are not correct.
- **do / doesn't not have to** is used to talk about something that is not our responsibility or is not necessary. There is no obligation.
- use **must not** and <u>not</u> *don't have to* to prohibit something, typically in instructions and notices that give warnings or very strong recommendations.
- there is no past form of **must not**, often **was / were not allowed** is used to express the concept of prohibition in the past.
- when giving instructions we often use *please don't* rather than *you mustn't*.

1. **Don't you have to / Haven't you to** stop off at Hong Kong when you fly to Sydney?
2. We **didn't have / hadn't to** drive because there was a great train service.
3. **Didn't they have / Hadn't they** to show any ID?
4. We **don't have to / mustn't** work tomorrow because it's a public holiday.
5. You **don't have to / mustn't** do it now, it can wait.
6. You **don't have to / mustn't** touch that it will give you an electric shock.
7. You **don't have to / must not** smoke in enclosed public spaces.
8. We **don't have to / must not** do this now, we can do it later.
9. She **doesn't have to / mustn't** prepare my lessons any more - she is very experienced.
10. You **don't have to / mustn't** say anything to him - promise me that you won't say a word.

1) don't you have to 2) didn't have to 3) didn't they have 4) don't have to 5) don't have to 6) mustn't 7) must not 8) don't have to 9) doesn't have to 10) mustn't

Chapter 35
Numbers, Dates and Measurements

They are about 50 km from here to there.

It is about 50 km from here to there.

A million euros are a lot of money.

A million euros **is** a lot of money.

We are leaving on the 21th of August.

We are leaving on the **21st** of August / on August **21**.

How did the exercise go? Well, I think I got the six wrong.

Well, I think I got the **sixth** (question) wrong.

There were two hundreds people at the concert.

There were two **hundred** people at the concert.

I got about the 50% of the answers correct.

I got **about 50%** of the answers correct.

He is tall one meter and eighty.

He is **one meter eighty tall.** He is **1.8 m tall.**

They won the match three at zero.

They won the match **three nil / three zero.**

© Springer International Publishing AG 2018
A. Wallwork, *Top 50 Grammar Mistakes*, Easy English!,
https://doi.org/10.1007/978-3-319-70984-0_35

Three hundred dollars is about three hundred and twenty euros.

Hundreds of people went on the demonstration.

Three **weeks is** a long time when you are in prison.

60 square **meters is** enough for me - I don't need much space.

It is **seven meters long / high / wide**.

Approximately 75% of Americans believe in alien abduction.

How is the test going? I am up **to number** seven.

Today is the **twenty third of May**. / Today is **May the twenty third**. / Today is **May 23 / 23 May**.

The final score was **three one** (3-1).

Guidelines

- When **hundred, thousand, billion** are preceded by another number (e.g. *three hundred*) no *-s* plural is required. You can say *hundreds, thousands* etc to mean *'several hundred / thousand'* (e.g. *Hundreds / thousands of people are becoming victims every day*).
- **Quantities** are considered singular (e.g. *three kilos is ..., 500 km is ...*).
- When referring to **measurements** note the word order: *I am two meters tall* (verb + measurement + adjective).
- The **definite article** (*the*) is not required before percentages (*the 10%*) or questions in a test (*I found the number three difficult*).
- **Dates** can be said in various ways. When writing it is best to avoid *-th, -st* and *-rd*, because you may attach them to the wrong number (e.g. *March 21th* instead of *March 21st* or simply *March 21*).
- **Sports scores** are said without a preposition: *We won six four* (6-4).

Choose the correct form

1. Two dollars **is not much / are not many** for a coffee.
2. The wall is **about four meters high / high about four meters.**
3. According to the survey, **about 60% / about the 60%** of people plan to vote for the Democrats.
4. **It is / They are** about 500 miles from here to Sacramento.
5. There were three **thousand / thousands** attendees at the conference.
6. **Millions / Million** of people are likely to become infected.
7. Real Madrid lost to Manchester United **four to one / four one**.
8. They are going on the **23th / 23rd** of December.
9. How did the exam ago? Well, I had some problem with the **eight / eighth** question and with **the question nine / question nine**.
10. 1.5 **kilo / kilos** of pasta **is / are** far too **much / many** for one person to eat at one meal.

1) is not much 2) about 4 m high 3) about 60% 4) it is 5) thousand 6) millions 7) four one 8) 23rd 9) eighth, question nine 10) kilos, is, much

Chapter 36
Passive vs Active

The accident was happened yesterday.

The **accident happened** yesterday.

The Second World War was broken out in 1939.

The Second World War **broke** out in 1939.

In her childhood she was undergone many hardships.

In her childhood she **underwent** many hardships.

In that area they are suffered from many natural calamities.

In that area **they suffer** from many natural calamities.

They were gradually disappeared into darkness.

They gradually disappeared into darkness.

In the book it is written that the prime minister knew nothing.

The book **says / states / claims** that the prime minister knew nothing.

© Springer International Publishing AG 2018
A. Wallwork, *Top 50 Grammar Mistakes*, Easy English!,
https://doi.org/10.1007/978-3-319-70984-0_36

He **was suspected** of fraud. = They suspected him of fraud.

A new party **will be elected**. = They will elect a new party.

Your bike **may be stolen**. = Someone may steal your bike.

Many demonstrators **are killed** in riots. = The police kill many demonstrators in riots.

He **has been promoted** at work. = He received a promotion.

They **have promoted** the movie all over the world. = The movie is being promoted.

Guidelines

- The active form is created using **to have** + past participle, it is never formed with **to be**.
- **to be** + past participle is only used to form the passive (never the active) - for more details see BE VS HAVE (Chapter 10).
- The passive form tends to be used: 1) When you are more interested in the person or object that experiences an action than the person or object that performs the action e.g. *The New York stock exchange was founded in 1792.* 2) When you don't know or cannot (or don't want to) express who or what performed the action e.g. *Four hundred thousand credit cards are stolen every year.* 3) To describe processes e.g. *The chemicals are transported by truck and are then delivered to the factory.*

Choose the correct form

1. Fifty thousand copies **sold / were sold** last year.
2. The inflation **is / has** gone up.
3. The concept of a self-driving car is that the car **drives / is driven** itself, it **does not drive / is not driven** by the passengers.
4. He **is / has** bought himself a car.
5. It **decided / was decided** that the service should **discontinue / be discontinued**.
6. Your taxi **is / has** arrived.
7. She **was / had** taken to the airport.
8. The machine **was / had** stopped for repairs.
9. An important document **had / had been** lost.
10. It **agreed / had agreed / was agreed** to spread the redundancies over six months.
11. Your email **has forwarded / has been forwarded** to the marketing department.
12. The form should **complete / be completed** in black ink.
13. An analysis **was / had** carried out of the samples.
14. The photocopier **left / had left / was left** on all night.
15. It **had decided / had been decided** to try to impeach Trump.

1) were sold 2) drives, is not driven 3) has 4) has 5) was decided, be discontinued 6) has 7) was 8) was 9) had been 10) was agreed 11) has been forwarded 12) be completed 13) was 14) was left 15) had been decided

Chapter 37
People vs *Person; Men, Human*

The people in the office is friendly.

The people in the office **are** friendly.

Ten persons are coming to my party.

Ten **people** are coming to my party.

She spoke while all the other persons listened and then fell asleep.

She spoke while all the other **people** listened and then fell asleep.

Most of students have read this book.

Most students have read this book.

The most people that I know have stopped using Facebook.

Most people that I know have stopped using Facebook.

A drug addict is a man who is dependent on drugs.

A drug addict is **someone / a person** who is dependent on drugs.

I'm nothing other than a man, there is nothing I can do about it.

I'm only **human**, there is nothing I can do about it.

Who builds houses knows how to put up a roof.

People / Those who build houses know .. **Builders** know ... **A builder** knows ...

© Springer International Publishing AG 2018
A. Wallwork, *Top 50 Grammar Mistakes*, Easy English!,
https://doi.org/10.1007/978-3-319-70984-0_37

> **People / Those** who swim every day **tend** to be very fit.
>
> **Most people have** access to the internet.
>
> The **person** I spoke to the phone said that **they** didn't know what I was talking about.
>
> A politician is **someone** who ...
>
> I met this **person** at a party who was a politician.
>
> Trump is a dangerous **man**.

Guidelines

- **people** is followed by a plural verb. **persons** is generally only used in a very formal context e.g. when talking about the capacity of a lift (max. capacity 6 persons).
- Do not begin an affirmative sentence with *who* (~~Who teaches English knows many things~~) when you mean *a person who* or *those people who*.
- Do not use **man** (or *he, him, his*) to refer to a generic person, use **someone** or **person**, or on some occasions **human**. For more details see PRONOUNS (Chapter 40).
- To talk about a majority of people use this construction: **most** + type of person in plural form (e.g. most teachers, most politicians, most doctors). Only use **most of** when you are making a qualification: *Most of the teachers that I know are ... Most of the children who live near me are ...*

Choose the correct form

1. The people I meet on my travels **tend / tends** to be very similar to me - I think of **it / them** as friends.
2. There **was little / were few** people at the party.
3. **The most part of people / Most people / The most people / Most of the people** that I know voted for her.
4. He is rather shy and doesn't like it with **too many peoples / too many people / too much people** around him.
5. Our lawyer is quite a young **people / person**.
6. A doctor is **a man / a woman / a person / someone** who looks after patients who are ill.
7. Notice: This lift is only designed to carry eight **people / peoples / persons**.
8. She is only **human / a woman**, she cannot be expected to do 20 things at the same time.
9. **Who lives / Those who live / People who live** round here have to be very careful as there are a lot of break-ins.

1) tend, them 2) were few 3) most people / most of the people 4) too many people 5) a person / someone 6) someone (a person) 7) persons 8) human 9) those who live / people who live

Chapter 38
Present Perfect vs Past Simple

When have you seen her? This morning? Yesterday?

When **did you see** her? This morning? Yesterday?

He has left Shanghai for a long time.

He **left** Shanghai a long time ago.

I have come to Shanghai three years.

I **have been** in Shanghai for three years. / I **came** to Shanghai three years ago.

My email address changed, I will give you the new one.

My email address **has changed**, I will give you the new one.

They have moved here in 2018.

They **moved** here in 2018.

They have left a few minutes ago.

They **left** a few minutes ago.

From last week I have changed my class.

I **changed** class last week.

© Springer International Publishing AG 2018
A. Wallwork, *Top 50 Grammar Mistakes*, Easy English!,
https://doi.org/10.1007/978-3-319-70984-0_38

108

> I **worked** there *from* 2014 *to* 2017 (finished period).
>
> I **have worked / have been working** there *since* 2018 (unfinished period - I still work there).
>
> She **set up** the company *in* 2018. She **has set up** many companies *in the last ten* years.
>
> They **went** to the bar an hour *ago*. They **have been** at the bar *for* an hour.
>
> I **bought** these books at the new book shop. I'**ve bought** so many books that I don't know where to put them.
>
> *Last year* you **made** a lot progress. I can see that you'**ve made** a lot of progress *this year* too.
>
> The stock market **crashed** twice *last year*. The stock market **has crashed** twice *this year* and it's only August.
>
> We **have redesigned** our website - take a look at it. We originally **designed** it five years *ago*.

Guidelines

- Your choice of present perfect or simple past will often depend on the time expressions you use. In the examples in the grey shaded box above, these time expressions are in *italics*. See also Chapter 39.

<u>Don't</u> use the **present perfect** in the following cases:

- to talk about completed actions in the recent past (even one second ago) or the distant past.
- to say when something happened (e.g. *yesterday, last week, when she was at university, many years ago*) you must use the simple past and not the present perfect.
- with time expressions typically associated with the simple past: *yesterday, last night, a few minutes ago, in 1945, when, then, before, after* etc.

Choose the correct form. In one case both forms are possible.

1. I have been there two weeks **ago / before**.
2. They have **come back this morning / just come back**.
3. We've done two exercises **so far / this week.**
4. They've emailed five times **yesterday / in the last three hours**.
5. They **haven't done it last week / still haven't done it.**
6. They have worked here **in 2018 / since 2018**.
7. She has been a professor **for many years / in 2017**.
8. They have won all their matches **last season / this season**.
9. Were you **ever in Mongolia? / in Mongolia for your holidays**?
10. Have you seen her **today / yesterday**?

1) before 2) just come back 3) so far / this week 4) in the last three hours 5) still haven't done it 6) since 2012 7) for many years 8) this season 9) in Mongolia for your holidays? 10) today

Chapter 39
Present Perfect With *For* and *Since*

I am here since last week.

I **have been** here since last week.

I live here all my life.

I **have lived** here all my life.

She is living here since May / for several months.

She **has been living** here since May / for several months.

They have been here from yesterday.

They have been here **since** yesterday.

They have implemented this new policy since 2017.

They **implemented** this new policy in 2017.

© Springer International Publishing AG 2018
A. Wallwork, *Top 50 Grammar Mistakes*, Easy English!,
https://doi.org/10.1007/978-3-319-70984-0_39

I **have worked** here *for* six months. (NB Not: ~~I work here for six months~~).

I **worked** for Google *from* 2012 *to* 2017, *now* I **work** for Apple.

I **worked** for Google *for* six years.

I **have been working** in Apple *for* five years.

I **have been here** *since* 11 o'clock / *since* 2005 / *since* last week.

I **didn't study** English at school, but I **studied** French *for* five years.

I **have studied** English *since* I left school.

We **have been studying** English *for* many years.

Guidelines

- When talking about an action's duration use **for** if you talk about the period / duration of time, and **since** when you say when the action began. Examples:
  for six years, for a long time, for more than an hour
  since 2017, since January, since he joined the company
- When you talk about when something began (*since*) or its duration (*for*), you need to use the present perfect (e.g. *I have lived*) and not the present simple (e.g. *I live*).
- Note that **for** and **since** can also be used in a phrase that contains the past tense:
  I worked there for 10 years = now I work somewhere else.
  I have worked here since I left school (if I left school in 2015, I could say *I have worked here since 2015*. Consequently, *since I left school* is the equivalent of a precise time)
- Do not confuse **for** and **since** with **from**. Use **from** to talk about a range of time: *I worked there from 2015 to 2017. They studied from 9 until 10.*
- Note the difference: *I am here for a month* = My plan is to stay here for a month. *I have been here for a month* = I arrived here one month ago and I am still here.

Write *for* **or** *since* **into the spaces in 1-10, and choose the correct form for 11-20**

1. _____ about three weeks
2. _____ Monday
3. _____ a long time
4. _____ a year
5. _____ 2017
6. _____ my birthday
7. _____ last week
8. _____ the Middle Ages
9. _____ over a month
10. ____ too long
11. I **am / have been** here for six months.
12. I **know / have known** Mary since July.
13. She **has / has had** that house all her life
14. I **am / have been** here for a week and I'm leaving tomorrow.
15. I **live / have lived** here since I was born.
16. I **live / have lived** in a small flat near the center.
17. She **knows / has known** him all her life.
18. She **knows / has known** him very well.
19. They **are / have** been here for a month, they arrived last week.
20. We **introduced / have introduced** the new policy **since / in** May last year.

1) for about three weeks 2) since Monday 3) for a long time 4) for a year 5) since 2017 6) since my birthday 7) since last week 8) since the Middle Ages 9) for over a month 10) for too long 11) have been 12) have known 13) has had 14) have been 15) have live 16) live 17) has known 18) knows 19) are 20) introduced, in

Chapter 40
Pronouns

If someone is interested he adds his name to the list.

If someone is interested **they** can add **their** name to the list.

If **you** are interested then **you** can add **your** name to the list.

Someone had parked his car in the middle of the street.

Someone had parked **their** car in the middle of the street.

Someone called for you this morning but he didn't leave his name.

Someone called for you this morning but **they** didn't leave **their** name.

A man / woman called for you this morning but **he / she (they)** didn't leave **his / her (their)** name.

(On the phone) Who is speaking? I am Anna.

(On the phone) Who is speaking? **It's me (Anna). / This is Anna**.

The job is not as easy as someone might expect.

The job is not as easy as **you / one** might expect.

With this app the user can do x and he can also do y.

With this app **users** can do x and **they** can also do y.

With this app **you** can do x and **you** can also do y.

© Springer International Publishing AG 2018
A. Wallwork, *Top 50 Grammar Mistakes*, Easy English!,
https://doi.org/10.1007/978-3-319-70984-0_40

If **someone** has a commercial activity **they** will suffer in an economic crisis.

If **you** have a commercial activity **you** will suffer in an economic crisis.

People who have a commercial activity will suffer in an economic crisis. **They** will find it hard.

Someone rang but **they** didn't leave **their** name.

A **man (woman)** rang but **he (she)** didn't leave **his (her)** name.

The user has to insert **their (his/her)** password before accessing the site. = **Users** have to **insert** their ...

If you have a **lawyer** then you can ask **them** for an opinion.

She has just had a baby. **Is it** a boy or a girl? **It's** a girl.

One never knows what **one's** future will hold, does **one**? (very formal, pompous, archaic)

You never know what **your** future will hold, do **you**? (normal form)

Guidelines

- **he (him, his)** should never be used as a generic pronoun, e.g. to refer to a generic lawyer, engineer, doctor etc. These are all jobs that can be done by women too. So use **they, them, their**.
- When **someone** (meaning one particular person) is the subject of the sentence, use **they** as the pronoun; however if **someone** refers to a generic person (i.e. everyone in such a situation), then prefer **you**.
- When asking the sex of a child or an animal use **it**. Also use **it** to refer to someone unseen: *I can hear someone in the next room, I wonder who it is.*
- When announcing who you are on the phone, use **this** or **it**: *This is John speaking. It's John here.*
- The impersonal pronoun **one** is very formal, prefer **you**.
- In written documents avoid using **he / she** by making the subject plural and using **they**. In any case, even with a singular subject (e.g. *the user*) you can still use the plural pronoun (*they, them, their*).

Choose the correct form

1. Someone telephoned for you while you were out, but **he / they** didn't leave **his / their** name.
2. If you know a person well, then you can tell **him / them** what you really think.
3. Somebody knocked at the door and then **he / they** went away.
4. The user then clicks on the icon. A menu opens and **he / she / he/she / they** can then see the various options.
5. A: Do you have a doctor? B: Yes. A: Well ask **him / them** what **he thinks / they think**.
6. In this class if **someone has / you have** a problem, **he / they / you** can ask the teacher.
7. If **one has / you have** a problem, **one / you** can ask the teacher for help.
8. Someone is at the door, go and see who **it / he** is.

1) they, their 2) them 3) they 4) they (he / she) 5) them, they think 6) you have, you 7) you have, you 8) it

Chapter 41
So, Too, Very, That + Adjective

My job is not so interesting.

My job is not **that / very / particularly** interesting.

They are not so big companies.

They are **not very / particularly** big companies.

The film was too good.

The film was **very / really / incredibly** good.

Sorry but this food is too for me.

Sorry but this is **too much food** for me.

Sorry, but I don't agree with you. The book was not so interesting.

Sorry, but I don't agree with you. The book was not **that** interesting.

© Springer International Publishing AG 2018
A. Wallwork, *Top 50 Grammar Mistakes*, Easy English!,
https://doi.org/10.1007/978-3-319-70984-0_41

The film is **very good** - I recommend it.

The film is **so good** that I think everyone should see it.

She is a really great actress. She is **too good** to be in a B movie like that. The movie was terrible.

A: The film was absolutely fantastic. B: No, I didn't think it was **that good.**

Guidelines

- **very + adjective** expresses approval and maybe followed by some other compliment or positive aspect e.g. *You are very good students - it's a pleasure to teach you.*
- **so + adjective** expresses great approval and often suggests a possible consequence e.g. *You are so good that I think you could actually be teaching the class!*
- **too + adjective** indicates that there is an excess of something. This excess can be negative (e.g. *This exercise is too hard*) or potentially positive (e.g. *You are too good for this class, I think I need to put you in a higher level*).
- **that + adjective** is often used to qualify or contradict what someone has just said e.g. *A: You are an excellent student. B: I don't think I am that good - I make lots of mistakes.*
- **too much / many** indicates an excess quantity of something, but without necessarily pointing at a consequence e.g. *I drank too much wine and ate too many cakes.*
- **so much / many** indicates a big quantity that generally has a consequence e.g. *I drank so much wine and had so many cakes that I was ill.*
- **that much** is often used to qualify or contradict what someone has just said e.g. *I don't think you had that much mine or even ate that many cakes - I don't know what you are talking about.*

Choose the correct form

1. You are a **very / so / too / that** beautiful person. I will never forget you.
2. A: You are **very / so / too / that** beautiful to work in an office you should be a model. B: You are **very / so / too / that** sexist, I can't believe you just said that.
3. They give us **very / so / too / that** much work but they pay us well.
4. They give us **very / so / too / that** much work that sometimes I have to work till midnight to get it finished.
5. They don't give us **very / so / too / that** much work, in fact sometimes we hardly have anything to do.
6. There are **very / so / too / that** many things I want to tell you, I don't know where to start.
7. There are **very / so / too / that** many things to tell you now, we don't have enough time.
8. A: He gave a great performance. I really enjoyed the play. B: I'm sorry but if he was **very / so / too / that** good why did he forget his lines?
9. Don't give me **very / so / too / that** much wine or I will get drunk.
10. A: So, over a thousand people work in that company, that's **very / so / too / that** large, isn't it? B: Well actually it's not **very / so / too / that** large, it's quite normal for an engineering company.
11. You are **very / so / too / that** lucky to have such a job.
12. He's not **very / so / too / that** good at this job, I wouldn't be surprised if he loses it.

1) very 2) too, so 3) too 4) so 5) that 6) so 7) too 8) that 9) too (so) 10) very, that 11) very / so 12) very / that

Chapter 42
So, Such, So Many, So Much

He is a such nice person.

He is **such a nice** person.

I didn't have so great expectations.

I didn't have **such** great expectations.

It is not so strong accent.

It is not **such a** strong accent.

It was a so short time.

It was **such a** short time.

I have so things to do.

I have **so many** things to do.

A. Wallwork, *Top 50 Grammar Mistakes*, Easy English!,
https://doi.org/10.1007/978-3-319-70984-0_42

> You are **so intelligent** that you could do any job.
>
> You are **such an intelligent woman**.
>
> You are **such intelligent women**.
>
> I have **so much work** to do, I don't know how I will manage. = I have **such a lot of work** to do, I don't know how I will manage.

Guidelines

- **so** + adjective + **that** + consequence e.g. *Your English is so good that you could do the exam tomorrow.*
- **such** + adjective + uncountable noun e.g. *You speak such good English.*
- **such** + **a** + adjective + singular countable noun e.g. *You have such a beautiful face.*
- **such** + adjective + plural noun e.g. *You are such wonderful students.*
- **so much** + uncountable noun e.g. *so much information / progress / money / evidence.*
- **so many** + plural noun e.g. *so many exams / students / books / houses.*
- **such a lot** + noun e.g. *such a lot of money, such a lot of books.*

See **COUNTABLE AND UNCOUNTABLE NOUNS** (Chapter 20).

Choose the correct form

1. They are **so / such** good teachers.
2. Her accent is **so / such** strong that I can't understand it.
3. She has **a so strong / such a strong** accent that I can't understand it.
4. This **job is so easy / is a such easy job** that anyone could do it.
5. I had never met **a so friendly / such a friendly** person.
6. There is so **much / many** information here that I can't understand it.
7. There is **so / such** a lot of information here that I can't understand it.
8. We had **a so good / a such good / such a good** time at the party.
9. I am in **so many / such a lot of** trouble, I don't know what to do.
10. I have heard **so / such** a lot about you. And I have heard so **much / many** about you too.

1) such 2) so 3) such a strong 4) job is so easy 5) such a friendly 6) much 7) so 8) such a good 9) such a lot of 10) such, much

Chapter 43
Some, Any and Related Issues

Any bread is in the freezer.

There **isn't any** bread in the freezer.

I have not wine, only beer.

I have **no wine / I don't have any wine**, only beer.

No one of the books is useful.

None of the books **are** useful.

I did nothing of interesting at the weekend.

I did **nothing interesting** at the weekend.

Could I have any more milk please?

Could I have **some** more milk please?

I couldn't answer no questions. They were impossible.

I couldn't answer **any** of the questions.

© Springer International Publishing AG 2018
A. Wallwork, *Top 50 Grammar Mistakes*, Easy English!,
https://doi.org/10.1007/978-3-319-70984-0_43

126

> There is **some wine** in the fridge but there isn't **any beer**.
>
> Would you like **some more wine**?
>
> I know you don't drink alcohol, but do you happen to have **any wine**?
>
> If you have **any queries** or need **any further** info, please let me know.
>
> I couldn't answer **any of the questions,** not a single one.
>
> I couldn't answer **some of the questions,** but most were quite easy.
>
> **None of the questions** were difficult to answer.
>
> **Nothing extraordinary** ever happens to me, although **something interesting** did happen this weekend.
>
> We have **no problems** at the moment.

Guidelines

The following guidelines are also <u>generally</u> true for derivatives of **some** and **any**, e.g. *anything, somewhere.*

- **some**: affirmative phrases (*I have some problems*).
- **some**: offers (*Would you like some coffee?*), and requests when the expected answer is 'yes' (*Could I have some milk please*).
- **some**: in negative phrases when the sense is 'a few' or 'a little': *I didn't understand some of what he said, but most of it made sense.*
- **any**: negative phrases (*I didn't understand anything of what he said - he was incomprehensible*).
- **any**: phrases and questions when you are not sure how the person will answer (*If you any problems, let me know. I know they are not in season but do you have any strawberries?*) In the two examples the writer / speaker doesn't know if the listener will have problems or will have strawberries.
- When **something** and **nothing** are followed by an adjective no *of* is required: *Do you have any ~~of~~ interesting to tell me?*
- Use **none** not **any** at the beginning of a sentence when the sentence is negative (*none of my teachers are good at their job - ~~any of my teachers~~*).
- Use **no** or **not any** but not **not** before a noun: *we have no milk, we don't have any milk, ~~we have not milk.~~*

Choose the correct form

1. Could you give me **any / some** help with my suitcases.
2. **Did you have** any / some **problems finding us?**
3. For **any / some** reason my last email had delivery problems.
4. Can I have **any / some** water please?
5. Is there **anything / something** you're not quite clear about?
6. Sorry, but **anyone / someone** is waiting for me.
7. Sorry, I've just seen **anyone / someone** I know.
8. **Anything / Something** has come up, so I'm afraid I can't come to the party.
9. We learn **nothing interesting / nothing of interesting** in his lessons.
10. We **have not bidets / have no bidets / don't have bidets** in our country.

1) some 2) any 3) some 4) some 5) anything 6) someone 7) someone 8) something
9) nothing interesting 10) don't have bidets (have no bidets)

Chapter 44
Stop, Remember

We stopped the car for looking at the accident.

We stopped the car **to look** at the accident.

I stopped to listen to the music on full volume as soon as my parents came here.

I stopped **listening** to the music on full volume as soon as my parents came here.

Don't worry - I remembered posting your letter, they said it should arrive on Monday.

Don't worry - I remembered **to post** your letter, they said it should arrive on Monday.

They stopped themselves at the motorway cafe to get some food.

They **stopped at** the motorway cafe to get some food.

I stopped to go to the disco when I was in my mid 20s.

I stopped **going** to the disco when I was in my mid 20s.

© Springer International Publishing AG 2018
A. Wallwork, *Top 50 Grammar Mistakes*, Easy English!,
https://doi.org/10.1007/978-3-319-70984-0_44

> I **stopped to look** at the shop windows. (I interrupted what I was doing before).
>
> I **stopped looking** at FB when the boss came in. (I was looking at FB before he came in).
>
> I **remember going** to the post office. (I recall the moment in which I went).
>
> I **remembered to go** to the post office. (I didn't forget).

Guidelines

- **to stop** + *-ing* = to interrupt a continuous activity (e.g. *I stopped smoking last year*).
- **to stop** + infinitive = to interrupt one activity in order to be able to start a new (e.g. *I stopped to tie my shoelace*, i.e. I was walking along the street and I had to stop so that I could deal with my shoelaces).
- **to stop** is not generally reflexive: *We stopped to get gas*. Not: *We stopped ourselves to get gas.*
- **to remember doing something** = to recall and visualize the moment in which you did / were doing something.
- **to remember to do something** = not to forget to do a task.

Choose the correct form

1. I stopped **to pick / picking** up some dinner for us.
2. She stopped **to help / helping** us change the wheel on our car.
3. She stopped **to help / helping** us when she realised that we could do everything by ourselves.
4. We had to stop **to fill / filling** up with gas - we had nearly run out.
5. We stopped on our way **looking / to look** at the new theatre.
6. I remember **telling / to tell** her because she reacted quite badly.
7. Will you remember **turning / to turn** off all the lights please?
8. We remembered **to go / going** to the supermarket - so we got the milk and everything else.
9. I remember her **to say / saying** that she never wanted to see him again.
10. Did you remember **to bring / bringing** my clothes?

1) to pick 2) to help 3) helping 4) to fill 5) to look 6) telling 7) to turn 8) to go 9) saying 10) to bring

Chapter 45
Used To and Present Tense

She is used to get up early - six o'clock every morning.

She **usually gets** up early - six o'clock every morning.

She uses to go to work by train.

She **goes** to work by train.

I am used to go to the sea for my holidays.

I **usually go** to the sea for my holidays.

We were always used to spend a lot of time together.

We **always used to spend** a lot of time together.

I read books from start to finish. I am used to do this way.

I read books from start to finish. **This is what I (usually, generally, always, often) do.**

In former / past times I went to work by bike.

I **used to go** to work by bike.

© Springer International Publishing AG 2018
A. Wallwork, *Top 50 Grammar Mistakes*, Easy English!,
https://doi.org/10.1007/978-3-319-70984-0_45

> **I (usually) watch** German films rather than American films.
>
> **She (usually) goes** to bed after midnight.
>
> **I used to watch** American films when I was a student.
>
> **I used to smoke** 50 a day now I only smoke 5 a day.
>
> **I (usually) get** up early. It suits me

Guidelines

- The simple present in English is used to express habits, things that you do regularly. So if you are talking about when you get up, how you get to work, when and what you eat etc, then simply use the present tense and combine it with an adverb e.g. usually, generally, normally. The form ~~I am used to get up at 7, she is used to have breakfast~~ etc does not exist. Instead you say: *I (usually) get up at 7. She (usually) has breakfast.*
- To talk about a habit in the past, then you can use: **I used to + infinitive**. This form implies that you no longer have this habit. Note that the verb *to be* is not used with this form: *I used to smoke*, not ~~I was used to smoke~~.

Choose the correct form

1. I **spend / use to spend** three hours studying every evening.
2. She **uses to send / sends** her children to bed early.
3. **I am used to watch / I usually watch** English movies with subtitles.
4. **I was used / I used** to spend three hours studying every evening, now I only spend two.
5. When I was a child, we **used to go / were used to go** on holiday to the mountains.
6. **We don't use to / We don't do** this in our country.
7. In some places **they use to eat / they eat** horses, but not here.

1) spend 2) sends 3) I usually watch 4) I used 5) used to go 6) we don't do this 7) they eat

Chapter 46
Very Much, A Lot: Use at the End of a Phrase

A doctor earns very much.

A doctor earns **a lot**.

I spent very much.

I spent **a lot**.

Before playing an energetic sport you need to warm up very much.

Before playing an energetic sport you need to warm up **a lot**.

I like a lot this movie.

I like **this movie a lot**. I **very much like** this movie.

She laughs very much - nearly all the time in fact.

She laughs **a lot** - nearly all the time in fact.

© Springer International Publishing AG 2018
A. Wallwork, *Top 50 Grammar Mistakes*, Easy English!,
https://doi.org/10.1007/978-3-319-70984-0_46

I love you **a lot / very much**.

I like my job **very much / a lot**. I **very much** like my job. I **really** like my job.

He plays tennis **a lot.**

She talks **a lot**.

I didn't spend **very much / a lot**.

Guidelines

- The meaning of **a lot** and **very much** is basically the same: a big amount. **a lot** is quantitative - this means that **a lot** could also be replaced with a number or a frequency. Look at these sentences: *She eats a lot. She talks a lot. He smokes a lot. He complains a lot.* You could replace *a lot* with: she eats *four meals day*, she talks *all the time*, he smokes *50 cigarettes a day*, he complains *every time he has a problem.*
- **very much** is qualitative and cannot be used when a quantity or frequency is implicitly involved. You can use **very much** generally with regard to describing your feelings about something or someone, typically with *love* and *miss*, and generally also with *like.*
- You can put **very much** between the subject and verb: *I very much like red wine = I like red wine very much.* You cannot put **a lot** before an infinitive or the object of the sentence: I want a lot to go. I miss a lot him.
- There is no difference between **a lot** and **very much** in negative sentences. So you can say *She doesn't talk a lot* or *She doesn't talk very much* with really no difference in meaning.

Choose the correct form

1. He eats **a lot / very much**.
2. I like **very much your parents / your parents very much.**
3. I **really want to see you / want to see you very much**.
4. I didn't see her **a lot / very much** while I was in Canada.
5. They spend **a lot / very much** on wine.
6. We don't get to talk to each other **a lot / very much** at the moment.
7. I **am very much / really** missing you my darling.
8. She sings **a lot / very much** in the bath.
9. I talk to my mother **a lot / very much**.
10. I **a lot / very much** want to see you.
11. Thanks **a lot / very much.**

1) a lot 2) your parents very much 3) really want to see you (very much = too formal in this context) 4) a lot / very much 4 5) a lot 6) a lot / very much 7) really very much = too formal in this context) 8) a lot 9) a lot 10) very much 11) a lot / very much

Chapter 47
Want, Would, Would Like, Would Prefer

She wants that I study more.

She wants **me to study** more.

They wanted that I went to university.

They wanted **me to go** to university.

They would want me to come with them.

They would **like** me to come with them.

She prefers that I remain with her.

She **would prefer me to remain** with her.

I would know if there are any seats available.

I **would like to know** if there are any seats available.

© Springer International Publishing AG 2018   137
A. Wallwork, *Top 50 Grammar Mistakes*, Easy English!,
https://doi.org/10.1007/978-3-319-70984-0_47

138

> I **want you to** study.
>
> They **want me to go** to New York.
>
> She **would prefer / would like us to** go with her.
>
> My parents **would like me to leave** home.
>
> I **would like to leave** soon.
>
> I **wanted to leave** the party because I was not enjoying myself.
>
> I **would leave** straightaway if someone could give me a lift me home.

Guidelines

- **want, would like** and **would** prefer require a particular construction: **to want +
  someone + infinitive**. Examples: *I want her to go. I would like them to come.
  I would prefer you to stay.*
- **would like** is often used as a kind of conditional form of to **want** (instead of
  would want). So when expressing a preference in a polite way you should say
  I would like you to go and not *I would want you to go.*
- When you say what you want someone else to do, say **I would prefer** and not
  I prefer. Example: *I would prefer you not to make such comments.* You use *I
  prefer* (i.e. the present tense) to talk about habitual preferences such as *I prefer beer to wine.*
- Do not use **would** when you mean **would like**. Use **would** to form the conditional
  of all verbs (*I would study more if I had time. She would go if you asked her*).
  Instead **would like** is used to express a preference: *I would like to study French.*

Choose the correct form

1. I want **that you / you to** tell me the truth.
2. I don't **want her to know / that she knows** anything about it.
3. I want **that there is someone that corrects me / someone to correct me** when
   I make a mistake.
4. My father wants **that I can / me to be able to** live independently.
5. I would prefer **my baby to sleep / that my baby sleeps** in another room.
6. I **prefer / would prefer** you to tell me now and not tomorrow.
7. I would really **like / want** you to sit next to me.
8. I would prefer **her not to hear / that she doesn't hear** about this.
9. I **would / would like to** try to summarize what I have been saying.
10. I **would / would like to** start again it if I were you.

1) you to 2) want her to know 3) someone to correct me 4) me to be able 5) my baby
to sleep 6) would prefer 7) like 8) her not to hear 9) would like 10) would

Chapter 48
Which? What? How?

Which kind of music do you like?

What kind of music do you like?

Which type of car does you father have?

What type of car does you father have?

Which do you want to drink?

What do you want to drink?

How is your name?

What is your name?

How is it called your cat?

What is your cat called?

What arm did you break?

Which arm did you break?

© Springer International Publishing AG 2018
A. Wallwork, *Top 50 Grammar Mistakes*, Easy English!,
https://doi.org/10.1007/978-3-319-70984-0_48

What do you like to drink at mealtimes?

Which do you prefer - red or white wine?

What type of music do you like?

A: I like jazz. B: Who do you like? A: I like John Coltrane. B: **Which** of his albums do you like the most?

What's the English for 'xyz'?

Which is correct? "I like very much you" or "I like you very much".

How do you say / pronounce 'xyz' in English?

How do you spell xyz?

Guidelines

- Use **what** to ask a generic question that doesn't distinguish between two or more items.
- Use **which** to discover a preference from a limited choice of items.
- Use **how** to discover the means with which something is done / said etc.

Choose the correct form

1. In need some shoes. **What / Which** size? **What / Which** color?
2. **What / Which** would you prefer - wine or beer?
3. **What / Which** is your favorite kind of music?
4. **What / Which** is your favorite pop band?
5. **What / Which** book do you want – this one or that one?
6. **What / Which / How** is this sport called?
7. **What / Which / How** is the name of this sport?
8. **What / Which / How** do you pronounce this word?
9. **What / Which / How** is the English word for *schadenfreude*?
10. **What / Which / How** do you say *schadenfreude* in English?
11. **What / Which / How** is your phone number?
12. **What / Which** is the best way to explain this to a child?

1) what 2) what 3) which 4) what 5) which 6) what 7) what 8) how 9) which 10) how 11) what 12) what

Chapter 49
Who, Which and *What* in Questions

What you did next?

What **did you do** next?

Who your son looks like? You or your husband.

Who **does your soon look like**? You or your husband.

What did happen next?

What **happened** next?

Who did build this house?

Who **built** this house?

Which club did win the most matches?

Which club **won** the most matches?

Which room does need painting?

Which room **needs** painting?

© Springer International Publishing AG 2018
A. Wallwork, *Top 50 Grammar Mistakes*, Easy English!,
https://doi.org/10.1007/978-3-319-70984-0_49

> Who **do you love**? I love my wife.
>
> Who **loves you**? My wife loves me.
>
> **Which company do you** work for? I work for Google.
>
> **Which company produces** the best software? Google does.
>
> I hear you did your cooking course yesterday. **What did you make?**
>
> **What made you** decide to do a cooking course?

Guidelines

- In the interrogative form, an auxiliary is normally required: *Who / What / Which did you see?* So the forms: ~~Who you saw? What you saw? Which you saw?~~ are not correct. However there are cases when the auxiliary is not required.
- Use **who / which / what + auxiliary** (e.g. *Who do / did*) when **who, which** and **what** are the object of the verb. In the question *Who do you love?* the pronoun *you* is the subject, and *who* is the object.
- Use **who / which / what + main verb** (e.g. *Who says .. Which costs ...*) when **who, which** and **what** are the subject of the verb. In the question *Who loves you?* the pronoun *you* is the object, and *who* is the subject.

Choose the correct form

1. Which film **did you watch / you watched** last night?
2. Who **did get / got** married?
3. Who **did you say / you said** got married?
4. What **does seem / seems** to be the problem?
5. Who **did say / said** that I was not coming to the party?
6. Who **did you go / you went** with?
7. Who **did go / went** with you?
8. **Which did come / came** first the chicken or the egg?
9. What **does turn / turns** you on the most?
10. What / Which courses **do you give / give you** the most credits?

1) did you watch 2) got 3) did you say 4) seems 5) said 6) did you go 7) went 8) came 9) turns 10 give you

Chapter 50
Will vs Present Simple

Can someone give me a hand with this? OK I help you.

OK I **will help** you.

Please can you send us further details. Of course, we send them later today.

Of course, **we'll send** them later today.

[The doorbell rings]. I go and see who it is.

I will go and see who it is.

When I will be 40 years old, I will probably ...

When I **am** 40 years old, I will probably ...

I wait here until you will get back.

I **will wait** here until **you get back**.

As soon as I know something, I tell you.

As soon as I know something, I **will** tell you.

© Springer International Publishing AG 2018   143
A. Wallwork, *Top 50 Grammar Mistakes*, Easy English!,
https://doi.org/10.1007/978-3-319-70984-0_50

144

> Your mobile is ringing. OK **I'll answer** it.
>
> I can't find my wallet. **I'll help** you find it.
>
> As **you will see** from the attached doc …
>
> **I'll contact** our HR manager and ask her to mail you.
>
> I'm sure Russia **won't win** the World Cup.
>
> When I **see** her I **will tell** her. I **will do** it when I **have** time.
>
> If it **rains** I **will stay** at home.
>
> As soon as I **find out**, I **will let** you know.

Guidelines

- When you make a decision at the moment of speaking (particularly in response to a request), use **will**. Do not use the present simple (or present continuous or GOING TO - Chapter 9).
- **will** is typically used 1) to express a spontaneous decision or make an offer to do something (e.g. *I'll help you with your suitcase*); 2) in emails and letters to refer to attachments or say what action we intend to take (e.g. *I'll get back to you with the information you requested*); 3) to predict future events, based on personal intuitions (e.g. *I think they'll lose the election*).
- With *when, before, after, until, if* (i.e. words connected with time), use the present tense directly after the time word and **will** in the other part of the clause (e.g. *When / If I see her, I will tell her*). See Chapter 17.

Choose the correct form

1. We **let / will let** you know when we have more information.
2. Someone's at the door. OK I **go / will go** and see who it is.
3. **Does it rain / Will it rain** when we **are / will** be in England?
4. What would you like to drink? I **have / will have** a coffee please.
5. If it **is not / won't be** hot next week then I **don't / won't** go.
6. I need someone to do this for me. OK I **help / will help** you.
7. How many people **are / will be** there next week?
8. I **get / will get** back to you with more details as soon as possible.
9. When I **have / will have** enough money I **travel / will travel** round the world.
10. I **call / will call** you before I **leave / will leave**.

1) will let 2) will go 3) Will it rain, are 4) will 5) is not, won't 6) will help 7) will be 8) will get 9) have, will travel 10) will call, leave

Part 2
Revision Tests

Chapter 51
Revision Tests

Revision Tests 1

Each sentence contains a mistake. Correct the sentences and then compare your answers with the corrected versions given in the first subsection of the relevant chapter.

1 advise, recommend, suggest
Can you suggest me a place to go?
I advise to see a lawyer.
He recommended her to see a doctor.
I recommend to identify some key points to remember.
We suggest you to come with us.
They suggested to use Google Translate.

2 allow, enable, permit, let
It is not allowed / permitted to smoke in class.
The teacher lets us to talk during lessons.
They allow using the dictionary during the exam.
This enables to make multiple copies.
It is not permitted walking on the grass.

3 already, just, still, yet
Are you just here? You are a bit early, aren't you?
Are you yet here? I thought you had gone.
I haven't yet decided what to do.
They haven't still come - I am worried about them.
They are here yet.

© Springer International Publishing AG 2018
A. Wallwork, *Top 50 Grammar Mistakes*, Easy English!,
https://doi.org/10.1007/978-3-319-70984-0_51

4 articles: a, an

She has a Apple computer.
He has an university degree and a MBA.
He was driving without license.
She works in bank.
I came without ID.

5 articles: a / *an* vs one *vs* it *vs* genitive

Do you have one mobile phone? Yes, I have it.
Do you think that this year will be more active than the last one?
That isn't David's umbrella, the one of David is striped.
We didn't go to Sigmund's house, we went to the one of Petra.
Bill and Mary went to the movies. This one had already seen it.

6 articles: *the* vs zero article (Ø)

All you need is the love.
English were very shortsighted to initiate Brexit.
The drug is a serious problem in today's society.
He had short hair and the eyes were brown.
I am not able to decide which is sentence is correct.

7 be able, manage vs can / could

I am not able to decide which sentence is correct.
I have never can ski.
I will can pass the exam if I study.
It was a very long marathon but she could reach the end.
By searching the web, I could find all the info I needed.

8 be born, die

I am born in Rome.
She is born in March so she is a Pisces.
The baby will born next week.
They found him alone in the flat - he was died.
He was dead ten days ago.
She is dead since many years.

9 be going to

According to the forecast, it rains later this afternoon.
Do you tell me or not?
How do I eat this without a knife and fork?
When I get home I am making dinner and watching TV.
Will you have a shower? If not, I am going to clean the bathroom now.

10 be vs have

It's snowing outside and I have cold.
She has 10 years.
What day do we have today?
You have right.
Is there a computer at you?

11 be vs have as auxiliary verbs
Demand is decreased.
He is gone back to the hotel.
She was arrived an hour before.
The lecture is begun.
Your child is grown a lot.
Your English is improved.
The director had made to resign.

12 been vs gone
I have gone to New York twice, the first time was in 2018.
He had already gone there, so he didn't want to go again.
Have you ever gone to Paris?
I have never gone to Venice.
You are late where have you gone?

13 can vs may
As you can remember, I have always loved jazz.
May you help me with my suitcases?
Someone can object if it's not true.
The woman in the picture can be a manager.
It may be that they have lost our address.
He can be in his late 20s.
I can say that it was very expensive.

14 cannot vs may not
I can not to see very well.
They can be annoying for me but cannot be for you.
She said she was rather busy, so she said she cannot come to the party, but let's hope she does.
It can be that I don't have enough money to pay the bill.
I may not come to the party - I am afraid I will be away that weekend.

15 collective nouns
Manchester United is playing Real Madrid tonight.
The police is investigating the case.
None of the books is worth reading.
The staff is having a meeting at the moment.
The gang is fighting each other.

16 comparisons
She is the better in the class.
I am worst than you at English.
It was the more expensive I could find.
This exercise is more easy than that one.
The new reservoir holds ten times water as much as the old one.
Bigger the mistake more you learn.
Her mother is a taller woman.
They came as late as midnight.

17 conditionals: zero, first (if vs when)
If I see her, I tell her what you said.
You will not pass the exam if you will not study.
When you arrive late to a Keith Jarrett concert they don't let you in.
I will call the police when she is not back within the next hour.
When I decide to go to New York this year, I will certainly come and see you.

18 conditionals: second, third
If my parents would give me the money I would go on holiday.
We would have arrived much earlier if we would not have got lost.
If I had not got married so young it was better.
If I would live in the country, I would be happy.
I would die, if he had seen me like that.

19 continuous forms
He is thinking that politics is a waste of time.
The dog is smelling. She needs a wash.
She's talked on the phone all morning - when is she going to stop?
Last weekend I didn't do anything because my girlfriend worked.
We went for a walk but after an hour it was raining.

20 countable and uncountable nouns
Excuse me, is there a news for me?
The news about her aunt are not good.
He has such a bad taste.
He's losing his hairs with all this stress.
I asked a staff at the informations desk.
I have a lot of experiences in writing reports.
Look at the damages she has done to our car.
They have done many researches on this.
This may be an evidence against astrology.
We went to the mall, had a lunch, and then saw a movie.

21 each, every, all, none
Almost each family has a fiber optic connection now.
Each of the students were afraid.
All of the students were not afraid.
Each of us did not have an umbrella.
Everyone are happy with the pay rise.
The prices are low for every goods.
These oranges are $1 for each.

22 few, little, a few, a little
Few days ago I met him at the station.
With the few money they gave me I was unable to buy fresh food.
He knows a little about this subject, almost nothing in fact.
Little people have seen this film.
We only have a few informations on this.

23 (this is the) first / second / third time
This is only the second time I try Chinese food.
This is the first time we are all together.
This is the first time I am taking a language course.
It was the first time I traveled by plane.
Is this the first time you come here?

24 genitive: the possessive form of nouns
This is the John's book.
The lesson of Tuesday is canceled.
The Trump's administration made many mistakes.
This is a typical everyday's problem.
This is an Alfred Hitchcock's movie.
I read a Harry Potter's book.

25 have, have got
Have you got a dog? Yes I've.
Do you have time? Yes, I have got.
Hypochondria is the one disease I don't have got.
I've a meeting in 10 minutes, have you got one too?
After buying the house, they had not very much money left.

26 have something done
I am not going to make cut my hair by my mum.
She is having her house to paint next week.
Do you make clean your house by an outside service?
I am having done my nails tomorrow.
I do get a lifting to my face.

27 how long, how much time, how many times
How long time do you live here?
From how much time have you been working for yourself?
How much time have you seen this movie?
How time do we have to do this exercise?
Who knows how long she is crying.

28 -ing form vs the infinitive
To cook is a very enjoyable activity.
After to teach you I will go home.
I look forward to hear from you.
While to watch the film I fell asleep.
How long will it take for reaching the next town?

152

29 languages and nationalities
Did you learn the Greek at school?
He speaks a good English.
She doesn't know the English.
The Spanish is simpler than the English.
English are a strange race.
I met one English and one Dutch.
There were two Japaneses on the train.

30 like, love, prefer
Would you like going to the movies with me?
Do you like me to show you how to do it?
She doesn't like when I use a curse word.
They prefer living in the country more than living in a town.
I like smoke.
If you don't mind I would prefer going to bed.
I don't prefer to go now.
I don't like that he eats with his mouth open.

31 make vs let
She let us to leave early.
They let us to think that they were experts in the field.
They made us work on our own, which was great because we all like working independently.
He made me to study all the rules.
Do you make build your house by a construction company?

32 much, many, a lot of, lots of
I have much work at the moment.
How much times have you been there?
Was there much people?
You don't need many money to do this.
There are many evidences to support this view.
There are many softwares to do this.

33 must vs have to
I must change train in Rome - there is no train that goes direct.
I must be at work before 10 every morning - although my boss is quite flexible.
Have you to do it immediately?
I've to go now - sorry.
At our school we must arrive at 8.0.

34 must not vs do not have to
He was left a lot of money so he hasn't to work.
We have not to do a written exam, just an oral one.
Thank you but you hadn't to go to so much trouble.
You do not have feed the animals.
Haven't we to go now?

35 numbers, dates and measurements
They are about 50 km from here to there.
A million euros are a lot of money.
We are leaving on the 21th of August.
How did the exercise go? Well, I think I got the six wrong.
There were two hundreds people at the concert.
I got about the 50% of the answers correct.
He is tall one meter and eighty.
They won the match three at zero.

36 passive vs active
The accident was happened yesterday.
The Second World War was broken out in 1939.
In her childhood she was undergone many hardships.
In that area they are suffered from many natural calamities.
They were gradually disappeared into darkness.
In the book it is written that the prime minister knew nothing.

37 people vs person, men, human
The people in the office is friendly.
Ten persons are coming to my party.
She spoke while all the other persons listened and then fell asleep.
Most of students have read this book.
The most people that I know have stopped using Facebook.
A drug addict is a man who is dependent on drugs.
I'm nothing other than a man, there is nothing I can do about it.
Who builds houses knows how to put up a roof.

38 present perfect vs past simple
When have you seen her? This morning? Yesterday?
He has left Shanghai for a long time.
I have come to Shanghai three years.
My email address changed, I will give you the new one.
They have moved here in 2018.
They have left a few minutes ago.
From last week I have changed my class.

39 present perfect with *for* and *since*
I am here since last week.
I live here all my life.
She is living here since May / for several months.
They have been here from yesterday.
They have implemented this new policy since 2017.

40 pronouns
If someone is interested he adds his name to the list.
Someone had parked his car in the middle of the street.
Someone called for you this morning but he didn't leave his name.
(On the phone) Who is speaking? I am Anna.
The job is not as easy as someone might expect.
With this app the user can do x and he can also do y.

41 so, too, very, that
My job is not so interesting.
They are not so big companies.
The film was too good.
Sorry but this food is too for me.
Sorry, but I don't agree with you.
The book was not so interesting.

42 so, such, so many, so much
He is a such nice person.
I didn't have so great expectations.
It is not so strong accent.
It was a so short time.
I have so things to do.

43 some, any and related issues
Any bread is in the freezer.
I have not wine, only beer
No one of the books is useful.
I did nothing of interesting at the weekend.
Could I have any more milk please?
I couldn't answer no questions. They were impossible.

44 stop, remember
We stopped the car for looking at the accident.
I stopped to listen to the music on full volume as soon as my parents came here.
Don't worry - I remembered posting your letter, they said it should arrive on Monday.
They stopped themselves at the motorway cafe to get some food.
I stopped to go to the disco when I was in my mid 20s.

45 used to
She is used to get up early - six o'clock every morning.
She uses to go to work by train.
I am used to go to the sea for my holidays.
We were always used to spend a lot of time together
I read books from start to finish. I am used to do this way.
In former / past times I went to work by bike.

46 very much, a lot

A doctor earns very much.
I spent very much.
Before playing an energetic sport you need to warm up very much.
I like a lot this movie.
She laughs very much - nearly all the time in fact.

47 want, would, would like, would prefer

She wants that I study more.
They wanted that I went to university.
They would want me to come with them.
She prefers that I remain with her.
I would know if there are any seats available.

48 which? what? how?

Which kind of music do you like?
Which type of car does you father have?
Which do you want to drink?
How is your name?
How is it called your cat?
What arm did you break?

49 who, which and what in questions

What did happen next?
Who your son looks like? You or your husband.
Who did build this house?
Which club did win the most matches?
Which room does need painting?

50 will vs simple present

Can someone give me a hand with this? OK I help you.
Please can you send us further details. Of course, we send them later today
[The doorbell rings]. I go and see who it is.
When I will be 40 years old, I will probably ...
I wait here until you will get back.
As soon as I know something, I tell you.

Revision Tests 2

Follow the instructions for each exercise. Then compare your answers with the example sentences given in the second subsection of the relevant chapter.

1 advise, recommend, suggest

Underline the correct form

1. He suggested **she should / her to** see a doctor.
2. He advised **to see / her to see** a doctor.
3. I would advise you **to see / seeing** a doctor.
4. He suggested **us to** / that **we should** go out for a drink.

2 allow, enable, permit, let

Underline the correct form

1. Our parents **let us / us to** go to bed late.
2. The teacher allowed us **to use / using** a calculator during the exam.
3. This app enables **to order / you to order** a taxi.
4. They were allowed **to go / going** home early.
5. It is not permitted **to smoke / smoking** inside the airport.

3 already, just, still, yet

Insert *already, just, still,* or *yet* into the spaces.

1. Is it midnight _____? Time for bed then.
2. Is it midnight _____? I can't wait to open the champagne to celebrate the new year.
3. Have you finished _____? It didn't take you very long.
4. Have you finished _____? You seem to be taking a long time.
5. They have _____ arrived. Typical, they always arrive early.
6. They have _____ arrived. Go help them with their suitcases.
7. They haven't arrived _____. But I imagine they will be here soon in any case.
8. They _____ haven't arrived. Where are they? I hope they haven't had an accident.

4 articles: a / an

Insert *a* or *an* into the spaces.

1. This is _____ European law.
2. This is _____ EU law.
3. This is _____ universal problem.
4. This is _____ unusual problem.
5. He is _____ NBC player.
6. He is _____ notoriously good player.
7. You cannot enter the country without _____ visa or _____ permit.

5 articles: a / *an, one, it*

Insert *a, an, one* or *it* into the spaces.

1. I have bought _____ new car - it is self-driving.
2. They have two cars. She has _____ and her husband has _____.
3. I went to the shop to buy the new iPhone and I bought the last _____.
4. Do you have a self-driving car? Yes, I have _____.
5. Do you have _____ with you now? Yes, I do.
6. Have you found your mobile? Yes I have found _____.
7. This _____ is bigger than that _____.

6 articles: *the* vs zero article (Ø)

Insert *the* into the spaces where appropriate.

1. Make ____ **love** not ____ **war**.
2. ____ **L / love** she felt for him did not waver while he was away during ____ **war** in Afghanistan.
3. ____ **R / researchers** spend a lot of time in ____ **laboratory**.
4. ____ **P / pollution** is a serious environmental issue and ____ **pollution** we have here in China is about ____ worst in ____ world.
5. ____ **English** is spoken all around ____ world. ____ **English** themselves only represent about ____ 10% of ____ **native English speaking people**.

7 be able vs can / could

Where possible choose **can / could**.

1. I would like **be able to / can** speak Spanish but I have never **could / been able to** learn it.
2. When I was five I **could / can** swim very well.
3. When I lived in Manchester I **was able to / could** go and see the best concerts whenever I wanted to.
4. We **couldn't / were not able to** see because of the rain.
5. I **couldn't / was not able to** answer any of the questions.

8 be born, die

Insert the correct form / tense of *to be born* or *to die* into the spaces.

1. She ____ in 1997.
2. Her baby ____ in a couple of months.
3. He **is** dead. He ____ last year. He ____ for one year.
4. By the time the ambulance got to the scene of the accident he ____ .
5. He ____ a few minutes before the ambulance arrived.

9 be going to

Put the verbs in bold into *going to, will*, the present tense or the present continuous.

1. The piano **be** delivered this afternoon. I don't know where **put** it.
2. Tonight I **relax** in front of the TV.
3. She says she **be** a doctor when she **grow** up.
4. Sorry but I **tell** you now. Maybe I **find** the courage to tell you tomorrow.
5. According to the Bank of England, inflation **rise** 2% next year.

10 be vs have

Insert *is, are, has* or *have* into the spaces.

1. She ____ three years old.
2. You ____ right and I ____ wrong.
3. I ____ cold - what's the temperature in here?
4. I ____ a cold, in fact I think I am getting a temperature.

11 be vs have as auxiliary verbs

Insert *was, were* or *had* into the spaces.

1. The criminal ____ arrested by the police.
2. The police ____ already arrested the criminal twice before.
3. The project ____ finished on time.
4. The project ____ already finished when I joined the team.
5. Taxes ____ increased by 20% by the new government
6. The problems ____ increased over the last two years.
7. The patient ____ taken to hospital in an ambulance.
8. The father ____ taken the children to school.

12 been vs gone

Insert *been* or *gone* into the spaces.

1. He has ____ to China - I don't suppose we'll see him again for a long time.
2. He has ____ to China twice. He said it was fascinating and he can't wait to go back.
3. We had ____ home already, that's why you couldn't find us at the office.
4. We had ____ to the cinema three times that week, so we didn't want to go again.

13 can vs may

Insert *can* or *may* into the spaces.

1. I _____ come next Wednesday at 12 o'clock - so note that down in your diary.
2. He _____ come next week, but he's not sure at the moment.
3. (Friend to another friend) _____ you help me with my homework?
4. (Shop assistant to customer) _____ I help you? Do you need some assistance?

14 cannot vs may not

Insert *cannot* or *may not* into the spaces.

1. I _____ come to the lesson tomorrow because I am on holiday. = It is impossible for me to come.
2. I _____ come to the lesson – I will let you know later today if I can or not. = Perhaps I will not come.
3. She _____ be at home yet, she doesn't stop work until after 6 pm.
4. I would try ringing her later because she _____ be at home yet.

15 collective nouns

Underline the correct form

1. Most of the companies in the survey **has / have** an intranet.
2. England **has / have** a population of 54 million.
3. England **is / are** playing South Korea in the world cup semi finals.
4. None of the films I saw **was / were** any good.
5. None of the information **was / were** up to date.
6. The crew / team / staff / choir **is / are** all from Mexico.

16 comparisons

Choose the correct form.

1. Microsoft is **bigger / more big** Amazon.
2. FIAT is one of the **biggest / bigger** companies in Italy.
3. Mexico City has the second **largest / larger** population in the world.
4. She is by far the **more / most** productive person in the company.
5. Thailand's inflation rate is not as low **as / like / than** Japan's.
6. She doesn't have **as much time as / like / than** I do.
7. She has **less / fewer** time than me.
8. They **have the same** number of clients **as / like / than** us.
9. **The more / more** I see, **less / the less** I understand you

17 conditionals: zero, first (if vs when)

Put verbs in bold into the correct tense. At the moment the verbs are in their infinitive form.

1. If you **mix** red and green you **get** brown.
2. If you **arrive** late at my company no one **say** anything - it's all very easy going.
3. If I **arrive** late tomorrow my boss **will be** very angry - we have a meeting early in the morning.
4. I **(not) pass** the exam if I **(not) study**.
5. When I **see** her, I **tell** her. It **will** either be Monday or Tuesday next week.
6. If I **see** her, I **tell** her. But to be honest I (not) **see** her very often so I can't guarantee anything.

18 conditionals: second, third

Put verbs in bold into the correct tense. At the moment the verbs are in their infinitive form.

1. If I **know** the answer I **tell** you. But unfortunately I don't know the answer.
2. I **study** more if I **have** time. I have some many other things to do which take up all my time.
3. I **travel** more when I was younger if I **have** the money, but in reality I **be** a poor student!
4. If I **pass** the exam I **be** very happy, but unfortunately I **fail**.

19 continuous forms

Put the verbs in bold into the present simple, present continuous, present perfect, present perfect, past simple or past continuous.

1. He **have** two dogs. = He owns / possesses two dogs.
2. He **have** lunch with her today. = He has made a future arrangement to eat with her.
3. They asked me what I **do**. = They wanted to know what my job is.
4. They asked me what I **do** there. = They wanted to know why I was there at that particular moment.
5. As I **tell** you ... = I didn't finish what I wanted to tell you.
6. As I **tell** you ... = I finished what I wanted to tell you but now I want to refer to it again.
7. He **talk** on the phone all morning. (He is still talking now).
8. I **talk** to her and we've resolved the matter. (I am not talking to her now)
9. I **do** my homework that's why I am so tired. Mother: But have you finished it?
10. I **do** my homework so can I play now? Mother: That's great, of course you can.

20 countable and uncountable nouns

Choose the correct form.

1. The most important **feedback is / feedback are** the **feedback / feedback** you get day by day.
2. Can you give me **some / a** feedback on this doc?
3. I needed **some / a** - I needed a bed and a wardrobe
4. IKEA furniture **is / are** very cheap.
5. She's doing a **training / training course**.
6. **The paper / Paper** is becoming an expensive commodity.
7. She reads **the paper / paper** every day.

21 each, every, all, none

Insert *each, every, everyone, all,* or *none* into the spaces.

1. _____ correct answer is worth 10 points.
2. I know the name of _____ student in the school.
3. I could hear _____ word they said.
4. The train runs _____ three minutes.
5. _____ of the books is / are worth reading.
6. _____ of us had been there before. We had _____ been there before.

22 few, little, a few, a little

Insert *few, little, a few,* or *a little* into the spaces.

1. _____ people know this. = Hardly anyone / Almost no one knows about this.
2. _____ people know this. = Some people know this, but not many.
3. _____ has been done to help the poor. = Not enough / Very very little has been done..
4. _____ has been done to help the poor. = Something has been done, so a minimum amount of progress is being made.

23 (this is the) first / second / third time

Put the verbs in bold into the correct tense.

1. It is the first time that I **work** like this.
2. This is the third time that I **tell** you this rule.
3. This is not the first time that I **come** here.
4. It was the first time that I **work** like that. In fact, I had never worked so much in all my life.

24 genitive: the possessive form of nouns

Where appropriate, insert into the blanks an apostrophe 's to indicate that the genitive is required.

1. My wife writes **history** ___ books.
2. Look at this bookshelf. The books on the left are my books and those on the right are my **wife** ___ (i.e. books that she has bought).
3. My **sister** ___ husband is not coming to **tomorrow** ___ party.
4. I have many friends. I went to my **friends** ___ party (i.e. **Jack** ___ and **Jill** ___ party) last night.

25 have, have got

Choose the correct form.

1. Do you **have / have got** time for a drink? Yes, I do. Sorry **I've not / I haven't got / I don't**.
2. We **are having / having got** a party tomorrow at our house,
3. **She has / She's got / She's** two cars.
4. **Did you have / Had you** a good holiday?
5. I'm sorry I **didn't have / hadn't got** time to do the exercise.

26 have something done

Create complete sentences from the words below.

1. They / their house / **renovate** next month.
2. I / my hair / **cut** / yesterday.
3. We / someone / **paint** / the living room for us.
4. She / her tonsils / **remove** / next week.

27 how long, how much time, how many times

Insert *long, much time*, or *many times* into the spaces.

1. How ____ have you been living in London?
2. How ____ will you be staying here?
3. How ____ have you been to New York? I have been to New York six times.
4. How ____ do we have available? Just a couple of hours.

28 -ing form vs the infinitive

Put the verbs in bold into the *-ing* form vs the infinitive.

1. **Have** a good memory you need **do** a specialized course.
2. **Have** a good memory is really useful.
3. Before **use** it you need **attach** the headphones.
4. I look forward to **hear** from you.
5. We would like **inform** you that we have decided **accept** your proposal.
6. This programme allows you **write** spreadsheets.
7. I persuaded him **let** me use his mobile.

29 languages and nationalities

Insert *the* into the spaces where appropriate.

1. _____ English is a relatively easy language.
2. For some people, _____ English spoken in the UK is more pure than _____ English spoken in the US.
3. _____ English are a conservative race.
4. He comes from _____ Wales, he is Welsh, he speaks _____ Welsh. _____ Welsh are very patriotic.

30 like, love, prefer

Choose the correct form.

1. I like **to play / playing** tennis in the morning rather than the afternoon.
2. I like **to play / playing** tennis with Tom because I always win.
3. I don't **like it / like** when she beats me at tennis.
4. I would prefer **to play / playing** with Tom than with Rick.
5. I would prefer **not to / to don't** go alone.
6. **Don't / Wouldn't** you prefer to go out to dinner rather than cooking at home tonight?

31 make, let

Choose the correct form.

1. The mother **made / let** her son stay at home. he wanted to go out but she wouldn't let him go.
2. The mother **made / let** her son stay at home because he didn't want to go to school.
3. The teacher **made / let** the bad student **stay / to stay** behind after the lesson.
4. They made us **work / to work** more than twelve hours a day six days a week.
5. We were made **work / to work** twelve hours a day.
6. We were not **allowed / made / let** to go home unless we had worked twelve hours..

32 much, many, a lot of, lots of

1. I have _____ friends.
2. I don't have _____ enemies.
3. I have _____ time.
4. I don't have_____ time.
5. We have _____ information.
6. We do not have _____ information.
7. Does he earn _____ money?

33 must vs have to

1. According to students from last year, you _____ study a lot on this course.
2. My mother says I _____ eat all my vegetables.
3. Police officer: You _____ wear a seatbelt at all times.
4. So when you are in England next year you will _____ wear a seatbelt.

34 must not vs don't have to

1. You _____ come if you don't want to.
2. You _____ come before 6 o'clock or you will ruin the surprise.
3. You _____ smoke in a non-smoking compartment.
4. You _____ do a written exam, just an oral.

35 numbers, dates and measurements

Choose the correct form(s).

1. Three hundred dollars **is / are** about three hundred and twenty euros.
2. **Hundred / Hundreds** of people went on the demonstration.
3. Three weeks **is / are** a long time when you are in prison.
4. 60 square meters **is / are** enough for me - I don't need much space.
5. It is **seven meters long / long seven meters**.
6. Approximately 75% of Americans **believe / believes** in alien abduction.
7. How is the test going? I am up to **number / the number** seven.
8. Today is the May **23th / 23rd / 23**.
9. The final score was **three one / three to one** (3-1).

36 passive vs active

Convert sentences 1-3 into the passive form, and sentences 4-6 into the active form.

1. They suspected him of fraud.
2. They will elect a new party.
3. Someone may steal your bike.
4. Many demonstrators are killed in riots (by the police).
5. He has been promoted at work.
6. They have promoted the movie all over the world.

37 people vs person, men, human

Choose the correct form.

1. **Who swims / People who swim / Those who swim** every day **tend to** be very fit.
2. Most people **has / have** access to the internet.
3. The person I spoke to the phone said that **he / she / they** didn't know what I was talking about.
4. A politician is **someone / a man** who ...

38 present perfect vs past simple

Put the verbs in bold into the present perfect or past simple.

1. I **work** there from 2014 to 2017.
2. I **work** there since 2018.
3. She **set up** the company in 2018. She **set up** many companies in the last few years.
4. They **go** to the bar an hour ago They **be** at the bar for an hour.
5. I **by** these books at the new book shop. I **buy** so many books that I don't know where to put them.
6. Last year you **make** a lot progress. I can see that you **make** a lot of progress this year too.
7. The stock market **crash** twice last year. The stock market **crash** twice already and it's only August.
8. We **redesign** our website - take a look at it. We originally **design** it five years ago.

39 present perfect with for and since

Insert *for, since* or *from* into the spaces.

1. I have worked here _____ six months.
2. I worked for Google _____ 2012 to 2017.
3. I worked for Google _____ six years.
4. I have been working in Apple _____ five years.
5. I have been here _____ 11 o'clock.
6. I didn't study English at school, but I studied French _____ five years.
7. I have studied English _____ I left school.
8. We have been studying English _____ many years.

40 pronouns

Insert *you, your, he, his, she, her, it, its* or *they, their* into the spaces.

1. If someone has a commercial activity _____ will suffer in an economic crisis.
2. If _____ have a commercial activity _____ will suffer in an economic crisis.
3. People who have a commercial activity will suffer in an economic crisis. _____ will find it hard.
4. Someone rang but _____ didn't leave _____ name.
5. A man (woman) rang but _____ didn't leave _____ name.
6. The user has to insert _____ password before accessing the site.
7. If you have a lawyer then you can ask _____ for an opinion.
8. She has just had a baby. Is _____ a boy or a girl? It _____ a girl.
9. _____ never know what _____ future will hold, do _____ ?

166

41 so, too, very, that + adjective

Insert *so, too, very,* or *that* into the spaces.

1. The film is _____ good - I recommend it.
2. The film is _____ good that I think everyone should see it.
3. She is a really great actress. She is _____ good to be in a B movie like that. The movie was terrible.
4. A: The film was absolutely fantastic. B: No, I didn't think it was _____ good.

42 so, such, so many, so much

Choose the correct form.

1. You are **so / such** that you could do any job
2. You are **a such intelligent woman / such an intelligent woman**.
3. You are **so / such intelligent** women.
4. I have **such a lot / as so lot** of work to do, I don't know how I will manage.

43 some, any and related issues

Insert *some, any, none* or *no* into the spaces.

1. There is _____ wine in the fridge but there isn't _____ beer.
2. Would you like _____ more wine?
3. I know you don't drink alcohol, but do you happen to have _____ wine?
4. If you _____ queries or need _____ further info, please let me know.
5. I couldn't answer _____ of the questions, not a single one.
6. I couldn't answer _____ of the questions, but most were quite easy.
7. _____ of the questions were difficult to answer.
8. We have _____ problems at the moment.

44 stop, remember

Choose the correct form.

1. I stopped **to look / looking** at the shop windows.
2. I stopped **to look / looking** at FB when the boss came in.
3. I remember **to go / going** to the post office.
4. I remembered **to go / going** to the post office.

45 used to and present tense

Choose the correct form.

1. I **usually / use to / used to** watch German films rather than American films.
2. She **usually goes / uses to go** to bed after midnight.
3. I **use / used** to watch American films when I was a student.
4. I **use / used** smoke 50 a day not I only smoke 5 a day.
5. I **usually / use to / used to get** up early. It suits me.

46 very much, a lot: use at the end of a phrase

In which cases would *very much* be possible?

1. I love you _____.
2. I like my job _____.
3. He plays tennis _____.
4. She talks _____.
5. I didn't spend _____.

47 want, would, would like, would prefer

Choose the correct form.

1. I want **that you / you to** study.
2. They want **that I / me to** go to New York.
3. She would prefer **that we / us to** go with her.
4. My parents would **like / want** me to leave home.
5. **I would like to leave / leaving** soon.
6. I **wanted / would like** to leave the party because I was not enjoying myself.

48 which? what? how?

Insert *which, what* or *how* into the spaces.

1. _____ do you like to drink at mealtimes?
2. _____ do you prefer - red or white wine?
3. _____ type of music do you like?
4. A: I like jazz. B: Who do you like? A: I like John Coltrane. B: _____ of his albums do you like the most?
5. _____ the English for 'xyz'?
6. _____ is correct? "I like very much you" or "I like you very much"
7. _____ do you say / pronounce 'xyz' in English?
8. _____ do you spell xyz?

49 who, which and what in questions

Choose the correct form.

1. Who **do you love / loves you**? I love my wife
2. Who **do you love / loves you**? My wife loves me
3. Which company **do you work for / works for you**? I work for Google.
4. Which company **produces / does produce** the best software? Google does.
5. I hear you did your cooking course yesterday. What **did you make / made you**?
6. What **made you / did you make** decide to do a cooking course?

50 *will* vs present simple

Put the verbs in bold into the future (*will*) or the present simple.

1. Your mobile is ringing. OK I **answer** it.
2. I can't find my wallet. I **help** you find it.
3. As you **see** from the attached doc …
4. I **contact** our HR manager and ask her to mail you.
5. Interest rates **go** down if the Democrats **win** the election.
6. I **be** sure Russia **(not) win** the World Cup.
7. When I **see** her I **tell** her
8. I **do** it when I **have** time
9. If it **rains** I **stay** at home
10. As soon as I **find out**, I **let** you know

Appendix

Below are the indexes to two other books containing grammar and vocabulary exercises. If you are a student, you can use these indexes to find additional exercises. You can also use the link below to take you to you to English for Academic Research: Grammar, Usage and Style where you can find more detailed explanations to clarify certain difficulties connected to grammar and vocabulary:
http://www.springer.com/gp/book/9781461415923

English for Academic Research: Grammar Exercises Index

This index is by section number. Numbers marked in bold mean that the whole section is dedicated to this grammar item.

© Springer International Publishing AG 2018
A. Wallwork, *Top 50 Grammar Mistakes*, Easy English!,
https://doi.org/10.1007/978-3-319-70984-0

English for Academic Research: Vocabulary Exercises

Table of Contents

This table of contents refers to the chapter numbers.

2.17 despite, despite the fact, however, in any case, in spite of the fact, nevertheless, notwithstanding, still, yet
2.18 e.g., i.e.
2.19 e.g., for example, i.e., such as, that is to say, etc
2.20 eventual(ly), if necessary, in the end
2.21 in fact, instead (of), on the other contrary, on the other hand
2.22 Various link words 1
2.23 Various link words 2

Section 3 Nouns

3.1 base, basis
3.2 basis, degree, extent, level, region
3.3 capacity, competence, skill
3.4 chance, opportunity, possibility, probability
3.5 consideration, observation, remark
3.6 danger, hazard
3.7 dimension, size
3.8 measure, measurement
3.9 motivation, reason
3.10 replacement, substitute, substitution
3.11 requirement, request, query
3.12 Various nouns

Section 4 Prepositions

4.1 about, for, of
4.2 above, over, below, under, underneath
4.3 among, between, of
4.4 among, between, from, of, with
4.5 at, in, into, inside, to
4.6 at, to, Ø (no preposition)
4.7 at, to, towards
4.8 by, from
4.9 by, from, in, of, with
4.10 during, over, throughout
4.11 for, of
4.12 in, into
4.13 in, on
4.14 in, into, on, onto
4.15 with, within

Section 5 Verbs

5.1 affect, effect, influence, condition, interest
5.2 agree with, be in agreement with, match
5.3 allow, enable, permit, let, mean
5.4 analyze, elaborate, process
5.5 anticipate, bring forward, expect, forecast, foresee, predict
5.6 argue, claim, pretend
5.7 arise, raise, rise, lead to
5.8 ascertain, check, control, verify
5.9 assist, take part, participate
5.10 assume, hypothesize, suppose
5.11 assure, ensure, guarantee, insure
5.12 attempt, demonstrate, prove, show, test, try, try out
5.13 avoid, prevent
5.14 be concerned, cope with, deal with, focus on
5.15 be the result of, turn out, result, result in
5.16 be born, conceive, derive from, originate
5.17 bind, bond, bound
5.18 bring, cause, determine, give rise to, lead to
5.19 compose, comprise, consist, constitute, form, make up
5.20 condition, conduct, drive, guide
5.21 decline, decrease, go down, lessen, lower, reduce
5.22 degree, grade, level
5.23 demand, request, require, requirement
5.24 desire, want, wish
5.25 determine, cause, induce, lead to
5.26 depict, highlight, show, visualize
5.27 detect, discriminate, distinguish, identify
5.28 divide, separate, share, split
5.29 entail, imply, involve, mean
5.30 evidence, highlight, show
5.31 exclude, rule out, marginalize
5.32 expect, presume, suppose, wait for
5.33 experiment, experience, proof, prove, test
5.34 lack, miss
5.35 propose, recommend, suggest

Section 6 False Friends and Synonyms

Index

© Springer International Publishing AG 2018
A. Wallwork, *Top 50 Grammar Mistakes*, Easy English!,
https://doi.org/10.1007/978-3-319-70984-0